COLD WAR ESSAYS

GAR ALPEROVITZ was educated at the universities of Wisconsin and California. He received a doctorate in political economy from Cambridge University. Between 1964 and 1968 he was a Fellow of King's College, Cambridge. He has been legislative assistant to several members of Congress, and from 1966 to 1968 was also a Fellow of the Institute of Politics of the John F. Kennedy School of Government at Harvard. His *Atomic Diplomacy: Hiroshima and Potsdam* was published in 1965. Currently, Alperovitz is Co-Director of the Cambridge Institute in Cambridge, Massachusetts.

CHRISTOPHER LASCH, Professor of History at Northwestern, is one of the noted revisionist historians and the author of *The New Radicalism in America* and *The Agony of the American Left*.

GAR ALPEROVITZ

COLD WAR ESSAYS

With an Introduction by
CHRISTOPHER LASCH

Schenkman Publishing Co., Inc.
Cambridge, Massachusetts

Three of these essays were originally published in slightly different form in *The New York Review of Books.*

For Guillemette

CONTENTS

COLD WAR ESSAYS

I. PREFACE

These four essays, three of which originally appeared in *The New York Review of Books,* were written in the late 1960s, but they mark the course of a longer period of study of American foreign policy in general, and of the Cold War in particular, a period in which my ideas changed as I reflected upon the expanding stream of evidence.

The first essay in the collection, a review of a book by Allen Dulles, describes the "Berne Incident"—the kind of specific event that jarred my thinking when I began research ten years ago. Now, perhaps it may serve as a detailed illustration of one of the countless affairs which, once the basic Cold War policy assumptions were made, furthered the suspicion, countersuspicion, and self-fulfilling prophecies that have characterized much of the history of the last twenty-five years.

The second essay is an effort to outline the larger framework into which such incidents fit. It discusses the dynamics of Soviet-American relations in the early post-World War II years. These are commonly considered the first years of the Cold War, but in fact, as this and the following essays try to demonstrate, neither 1945 nor 1947 marks the earliest manifestation of the basic relationships.

The second essay also touches upon the role of power —specifically nuclear power—in the making of foreign policy. Possession of the atomic bomb, as I argue here, and as I have tried to show at length in *Atomic Diplomacy: Hiroshima and Potsdam,* gave American policymakers an exaggerated sense of confidence, particularly in their dealings with the Soviet Union. It served to continue, reinforce, and complicate the more irrational aspects of the general anti-Soviet policy that has been a touchstone of American diplomacy since 1917. And it helped to create what Sir Denis Brogan once called the American "sense of omnipotence."

The third essay in the collection discusses a slightly different—in fact, a reverse—question: How dropping the bomb was affected by policy considerations. The essay argues that there was no "decision" to use the atomic bomb. Instead, as many now see, the use of the bomb flowed out of the *momentum* of events, out of the locked-in quality of men (and institutions), who, once committed, saw no way to rearrange their priorities and decisions.

Most observers who recognize this point assume the momentum was a military one, generated in the rush to end World War II. To sharpen the main argument of the essay let me here stress that, although the word "momentum" may be helpful, the word "military" is not. By July 1945 none of the highest *military* officials argued that the bomb was necessary in order to end the war without a land invasion, although, of course, they had argued this view earlier in the spring of 1945. At the end of the summer, after new Japanese cables were intercepted, men like Leahy, Eisenhower, and even Le-May saw that the war could almost certainly be ended without an invasion. Moreover, there were still three months before the November date which had been set for the first landing during the earlier planning period. In this time the various alternative ways to end the war could have been explored without danger.

The question is: Why did the momentum remain when the military reasons disappeared? The third essay seeks to demonstrate in detail that the inability of policymakers to alter their assumption that the bomb would be used can be explained, after July 1945, only in conjunction with diplomatic plans related to the Soviet Union. In short, a *diplomatic* momentum had by this time taken control of policy.

The fourth in this brief series of essays attempts to put the anti-Soviet policy, the Cold War, and the War in Vietnam into the context of a much deeper American tradition. A major theme of the essay is that our repeated interventions—before, during, and after the Cold War—are best understood as products of our deeply expansionist institutions and traditions. Drawing on some of the lessons of the Cold War, the essay also hazards three conclusions about the future: first, that there is a tremendous need for the negative and essentially conservative work of halting the interventionist course of American policy; second, that this work will certainly go forward, and that it is likely to succeed—although over time and probably after a trying period of reaction; and third, above all, that there is a critical need for the positive work of attempting to change our basic attitudes and institutional arrangements—both simply to better the nation and also to destroy the mechanisms

3

that so regularly have expanded our commitments abroad, and have wasted our resources in sorry interventions on behalf of the commitments. As the reader will see, this essay also represents a partial revision of the views expressed in the earlier work—although I have reprinted the first essays in substantially their original form.

The fourth essay concludes the book and also my own research on foreign policy. Though I hope to help edit a reader and perhaps help devise some ways to constrain policy, by making it more responsive to popular sentiment, my judgment is that the last point of the fourth essay should be taken seriously. Hence, my future work will be concerned almost exclusively with domestic policy matters and with efforts to transform the political economy of our domestic institutions.

Two final remarks: I have included in this collection a brief appendix which contains an exchange of letters with Herbert Feis, Albert L. Weeks and others. These may serve to clarify some of the points brought out in the essays.

Finally, I wish to say that, although these essays are mainly by-products of research done in connection with my first book, my thinking is grounded in earlier years as a student—at the University of Wisconsin with William Appleman Williams, and at Cambridge University with Joan Robinson and E. H. Carr, all of whom I acknowledge and thank for ideas, criticism, and inspiration. For a sense of "how it really is," I am indebted to my former colleagues among the members and staff of the U. S. House of Representatives, Senate, and Department of State, and also to the Fellows of the Institute of Politics of the John F. Kennedy School of Government at Harvard University. For continuing stimulation, friendship, and criticism, I wish to thank

4

the Fellows of the Institute for Policy Studies. Especially in connection with the last essay, I am in debt to my friend Rhea Wilson. To Christopher Lasch my thanks for consenting to write an introduction to the essays. And, finally, I can here only acknowledge, rather than truly express, my gratitude to my wife Guillemette —for the help she has given in more ways than she knows.

GAR ALPEROVITZ

Cambridge, Massachusetts
December, 1969

II. INTRODUCTION

By Christopher Lasch

At Yalta, in February 1945, Winston Churchill declared that world peace was nearer the grasp of the assembled statesmen of the great powers "than at any time in history." It would be "a great tragedy," he said, "if they, through inertia or carelessness, let it slip from their grasp. History would never forgive them if they did."

Yet the Yalta agreements themselves, which seemed at the time to lay the basis of postwar cooperation, shortly provided the focus of bitter dissension, in which each side accused the other of having broken its solemn promises. In Western eyes, Yalta meant free elections and parliamentary democracies in Eastern Europe, while the Russians construed the agreements as recognizing their demand for governments friendly to the Soviet Union. The resulting dispute led to mutual mistrust and to a hardening of positions on both sides. By the spring of 1946 Churchill himself, declaring that "an iron curtain has descended" across Europe, admitted, in effect, that the "tragedy" he had feared had come to pass. Europe split into hostile halves, the eastern half dominated by the Soviet Union, the western part sheltered nervously under the protection of American arms. NATO, founded in 1949 and countered by the Russian-sponsored Warsaw Pact, merely ratified the existing division of Europe.

After 1946 every threat to the stability of this uneasy balance produced an immediate political crisis—the Greek civil war in 1947, the Communist *coup* in Czechoslovakia and the Berlin blockade in 1948—each of which added to existing tensions, deepened hostility on both sides, and increased the likelihood of war. When Bernard Baruch announced in April 1947 that "we are in the midst of a cold war," no one felt inclined to contradict him. The phrase stuck, as an accurate description of postwar political realities.

Many Americans concluded, moreover, that the United States was losing the Cold War. Two events in particular contributed to this sense of alarm—the collapse of Nationalist China in 1949 (followed by Chiang Kai-shek's flight to Taiwan) and the explosion of an atomic bomb by the Russians in the same year. These events gave rise to the charge that American leaders had deliberately or unwittingly betrayed the country's interests. The Alger Hiss case was taken by some people as proof that the Roosevelt Administration had been riddled by subversion. Looking back to the wartime alliance with the Soviet Union, the American right began to argue that Roosevelt, by trusting the Russians, had sold out the cause of freedom. Thus Nixon and McCarthy, aided by historians like Stefan J. Possony, C. C. Tansill, and others, accused Roosevelt of handing Eastern Europe to the Russians and of giving them a

8

preponderant interest in China which later enabled the Communists to absorb the entire country.

The liberal interpretation of the Cold War—what shortly became the orthodox interpretation—developed partly as a response to these charges. In liberal eyes, the right-wingers made the crucial mistake of assuming that American actions had been decisive in shaping the postwar world. Attempting to rebut this conspiracy theory of postwar politics, liberals relied heavily on the argument that the shape of postwar politics had already been dictated by the war itself, in which the Western democracies had been obliged to call on Soviet help in order to defeat Hitler. These events, they maintained, had left the Soviet Union militarily dominant in Eastern Europe and, generally, occupying a position of much greater power, relative to the West, than she had enjoyed before the war. In the face of these facts, the United States had very little leeway in determining events in what were destined to become Soviet spheres of influence, particularly since Stalin was apparently determined to expand even if expansion meant ruthlessly breaking his agreements. After all, the liberals emphasized, Stalin, not Roosevelt or Truman, broke the Yalta agreement on Poland, thereby precipitating the Cold War.

These were the arguments presented, often with great force, in George F. Kennan's *American Diplomacy;* in William McNeill's *America, Britain and Russia: Their Cooperation and Conflict;* in Norman Graebner's *Cold War Diplomacy;* in Louis J. Halle's *Dream and Reality* and *The Cold War as History;* and most important in Herbert Feis's series on the diplomatic history of the Second World War: *Churchill-Roosevelt-Stalin, Between War and Peace,* and *Japan Subdued* (subsequently revised as *The Atomic Bomb and the*

End of World War II and reviewed by Gar Alperovitz in the third of the essays in the present volume). All these writers saw containment as a necessary response to Soviet expansionism and the deterioration of Western power in Eastern Europe. At the same time, they were critical, in varying degrees, of the legalistic-moralistic tradition that ran "like a red skein," according to Kennan, through American diplomacy, and that prevented American statesmen from looking at foreign relations in the light of balance-of-power considerations.

Their criticisms of American policy, however, did not challenge the basic premise of American policy, that the Soviet Union is a ruthlessly aggressive power bent on world domination. The liberal historians assumed, moreover, that in 1945 the Russians were in a position to realize large parts of this program, and that only counterpressure exerted by the West, in the form of containment and the Marshall Plan, prevented the Communists from absorbing all of Europe and much of the rest of the world as well.

It is their criticism of these assumptions that defines the so-called revisionist historians of the Cold War and distinguishes them from "realists" like Kennan and Feis. What impresses revisionists is not Russia's strength but her military weakness following the devastating war with Hitler, in which the Russians suffered much heavier losses than any other member of the alliance. Beginning with Carl Marzani's *We Can Be Friends: Origins of the Cold War* (1952), revisionists have argued that Russia's weakness dictated, for the moment at least, a policy of postwar cooperation with the West. Western leaders' implacable hostility to Communism, they contend, prevented them from seeing this fact, a proper understanding of which might have prevented the Cold War. This argument is spelled out in D. F.

Fleming's two-volume study, *The Cold War and Its Origins* (1961); in David Horowitz's *The Free World Colossus* (1965), which summarizes and synthesizes a great deal of revisionist writing; and in the works of William Appleman Williams, particularly *The Tragedy of American Diplomacy* (1959), which not only challenges the orthodox interpretation of the Cold War but sets against it an elaborate counterinterpretation which forces one to see American policy in the early years of the Cold War as part of a larger pattern of American globalism reaching as far back as 1898. According to Williams, American diplomacy has consistently adhered to the policy of the "open door"—that is, to a policy of commercial, political, and cultural expansion that seeks to extend American influence into every corner of the earth. This policy was consciously and deliberately embarked upon, Williams argues, because American statesmen believed that American capitalism needed ever-expanding foreign markets in order to survive, the closing of the frontier having put an end to its expansion on the continent of North America. Throughout the twentieth century the makers of American foreign policy have interpreted the national interest in this light.

The Cold War therefore has to be seen, according to Williams, as the latest phase of a continuing effort to make the world safe for democracy—that is, liberal capitalism, American-style—in which the United States finds itself increasingly cast as the leader of a world-wide counterrevolution. After the Second World War, American statesmen were confident of America's strength and Russia's weakness (although later they and their apologists found it convenient to argue that the contrary had been the case). Furthermore, they believed that "we cannot have full employment and prosperity in the United States without the foreign markets," as Dean Acheson told a special Congressional committee on postwar economic policy and planning in November 1944. These considerations led to the conclusion, as President Truman put it in April 1945, that the United States should "take the lead in running the world in the way that the world ought to be run"; or more specifically, in the words of Foreign Economic Administrator Leo Crowley, that "if you create good governments in foreign countries, automatically you will have better markets for ourselves." Accordingly, the United States pressed for the "open door" in Eastern Europe and elsewhere.

Exactly how these basic assumptions of American policy contributed to the beginnings of the Cold War Gar Alperovitz explained, in detail, in his *Atomic Diplomacy: Hiroshima and Potsdam* (1965). That book, based on a mass of documentation untouched by earlier revisionist historians, made it difficult for conscientious scholars any longer to avoid the challenge of revisionist interpretations. Alperovitz showed that as early as April 1945 American officials from President Truman on down had decided to force a "symbolic showdown" with the Soviet Union over the future of Eastern Europe. Truman believed that a unified Europe was the key to European recovery and economic stability, since the agricultural southeast and the industrial northwest depended on each other. Soviet designs on Eastern Europe, Truman reasoned, threatened to disrupt the economic unity of Europe and therefore had to be resisted. The only question was whether the showdown should take place immediately or be delayed until the bargaining position of the United States had improved.

At first it appeared to practically everybody that delay would only weaken the position of the United States. Both of its major bargaining counters, its armies in Europe and its Lend-Lease credits to Russia, could be more effectively employed at once, it seemed, than at any future time. Accordingly, Truman tried to "lay it on the line" with the Russians. He demanded that they "carry out their [Yalta] agreements" by giving the pro-Western elements in Poland an equal voice in the Polish Government (although Roosevelt, who made the Yalta agreements, believed that "we placed, as clearly shown in the agreement, somewhat more emphasis" on the Warsaw [pro-Communist] Government than on the pro-Western leaders). When Stalin objected that Poland was "a country in which the U.S.S.R. is interested first of all and most of all," the United States tried to force him to give in by cutting back Lend-Lease payments to Russia.

At this point, however—in April 1945—Secretary of War Henry L. Stimson convinced Truman that "we shall probably hold more cards in our hands later than now." He referred to the atomic bomb, and if Truman decided to postpone the showdown with Russia it was because Stimson and other advisers persuaded him that the new weapon would "put us in a position," as Secretary of State James F. Byrnes argued, "to dictate our own terms at the end of the war." To the amazement of those not privy to the secret, Truman proceeded to take a more conciliatory attitude toward Russia, an attitude symbolized by Harry Hopkins' mission to Moscow in June 1945. Meanwhile, Truman twice postponed the meeting with Churchill and Stalin at Potsdam. Churchill complained, "Anyone can see that in a very short space of time our armed power on the Continent will have vanished." But when Truman told Churchill that an atomic bomb had been successfully exploded at Alamogordo, exceeding all expectations, Churchill immediately understood and endorsed the strategy of delay. "We were in the presence of a new factor in human affairs," he said, "and possessed of powers which were irresistible." Not only Germany but even the Balkans, which Churchill and Roosevelt had formerly conceded to the Russian sphere, now seemed amenable to Western influence. That assumption, of course, had guided American policy since April, but it could not be acted upon until the bombing of Japan provided the world with an unmistakable demonstration of American military supremacy.

Early in September the foreign ministers of the Big Three met in London. Byrnes—armed, as Stimson noted, with "the presence of the bomb in his pocket, so to speak, as a great weapon to get through" the conference—tried to press the American advantage. He demanded that the governments of Bulgaria and Rumania reorganize themselves along lines favorable to the West. In Bulgaria firmness won a few concessions; in Rumania the Russians stood firm. The American strategy had achieved no noteworthy success. But as Stimson, one of the architects of that strategy, rather belatedly observed, it had "irretrievably embittered" Soviet-American relations for years to come.

In the following essays Alperovitz elaborates on the argument of *Atomic Diplomacy*, not only by filling in chinks of the narrative history of American diplomacy in the critical year 1945—as in the essay on the "Berne Incident"—but by placing the history of the Cold War in the larger perspective of American imperialism. In the longest of these essays, "The United States, the

Revolutions, and the Cold War," he shows that active intervention against revolutionary change had become the established policy of the United States long before it was applied to Eastern Europe in the closing phase of the Second World War. That policy, Alperovitz argues, did not rest only on the need for raw materials and markets; while it may have begun as "dollar diplomacy," it soon achieved the status of a "moral mission" to stamp out political heresy. In other words, it assumed the form of a messianic ideology that acquired a force and persuasiveness of its own, quite independent of the political and economic interests underlying it.

Because the counterrevolutionary character of American diplomacy often clothes itself in the loftiest moral idealism, "the reality of American antirevolutionary policy," Alperovitz writes, "has been obscured . . . to most people." From Woodrow Wilson on, moreover, American imperialists have not only spoken the language of anti-imperialism but have found themselves in practical opposition to the imperialistic policies of other powers. American influence in the world has expanded not only at the expense of revolutionary nationalists in the undeveloped countries but at the expense of the older empires of Britain, France, Germany, and Japan. Thus —to cite a typical example of this process—one finds Patrick Hurley, Franklin D. Roosevelt's man in the Near East, writing to Roosevelt in 1944 that, whereas Britain's presence in Iran and the Middle East generally had always been associated with "the principles of imperialism, monopoly, and exploitation," the United States—by obtaining oil concessions that had formerly been awarded to the British—would uphold the principles of "liberty and democracy." Roosevelt, according to Cordell Hull, "was rather thrilled with the idea of using Iran as an example of what we could do by an unselfish American policy."

The objectives of this "unselfish" policy had already been spelled out in State Department directives instructing Middle Eastern embassies to "render all appropriate assistance to the representatives of American oil companies who may be seeking petroleum concessions" and in a State Department memorandum of April 11, 1944, which sought for the United States, "in the interest of security, a substantial and geographically diversified holding of foreign petroleum resources in the hands of United States nationals." Earlier Churchill had written to Roosevelt, "There is apprehension in some quarters here that the United States has a desire to deprive us of our oil assets in the Middle East. . . ." These fears were well founded. The decline of British power and its implications for American diplomacy were astutely assessed, early in 1945, by an American businessman, Lamar Fleming, Jr., whose letters were forwarded to the State Department. "British empire and British international influence is a myth already," Fleming wrote. After the war the United States would have to protect British interests against the U.S.S.R., and this meant "the absorption into [the] American empire of the parts of the British Empire which we will be willing to accept."[1]

Fleming had no scruples about speaking of an American empire, but in the minds of most Americans— including the policymakers themselves—American objectives almost invariably present themselves as the de-

[1] On the diplomacy of oil in the Middle East see Gabriel Kolko, *The Politics of War* (New York: Random House, 1969), Ch. 12, from which the information in the preceding paragraph is taken.

fense of "liberty and democracy." Yet, as Alperovitz shows, the defense of liberty has led to a series of military and political interventions in other countries, in which the United States, despite its ostensible commitment to social reform, usually finds itself on the side of reaction. The pattern is too consistent to be explained as accident. To be sure, American policymakers have made serious mistakes, and it is no part of Alperovitz's analysis to minimize the importance of those mistakes. He does not subscribe to the mechanistic theory of American imperialism, popular in some new left circles, which attributes to American policy an almost diabolical foresight and which sees every action as carefully plotted according to a blueprint for world-wide domination and at the same time "determined" by the underlying economic realities.

Alperovitz understands the connection between the ideology of American globalism and the expansive tendencies of American corporate enterprise, but he also understands the way in which "antirevolutionism has transcended its historical roots" and has led the United States to make political commitments that cannot be explained as the result of rational economic calculations and that are not even strictly necessary to their realization. Counterrevolutionary intervention, he insists, is not so much a master strategy as a set of patterned reflexes deeply rooted in powerful political realities. This fact—the reflexive, almost unconscious character of American diplomacy—helps to explain why the United States overreached itself in 1945 when it tried to force the Russians to accept a *cordon sanitaire* in Eastern Europe. The sense of American military power was so overwhelming, and the desire for a "showdown" with Russia so acute, that American policymakers adopted positions from which they were soon forced to retreat—just as, under somewhat different circumstances, they will have to retreat from their effort to prove in Vietnam that wars of national liberation cannot succeed.

In both cases American planners have become, to a considerable extent, the victims of their own ideology. Globalism tends to carry with it what Williams calls the illusion of American omnipotence. Likewise the rhetoric of anti-Communism, which Americans have used to give moral sanction to their interventionist diplomacy, often leads to illusions about the nature of the adversary. Throughout the Cold War the United States has made the mistake of taking Soviet revolutionary rhetoric at its face value, ignoring the degree to which the Soviets themselves, as an established power, have developed a strong interest in international stability. As Gabriel Kolko puts it, writing of events in 1945, "the Russians were as committed to revolution as the West was to democracy." A recognition of their mutual interest in counterrevolution might have furnished the basis for the spheres-of-influence policy advocated by Churchill in 1944—before he too fell under the spell of American omnipotence in the form of the atomic bomb. But American planners tended to share the view of Henry L. Stimson (June 1945) that "no permanently safe international relations can be established between two such fundamentally different national systems."

Later, as we have seen, Stimson appeared to change his mind. His earlier view, however, remained one of the basic premises of American policy. More than twenty years later Arthur Schlesinger echoes it when he writes that "postwar collaboration between Russia and America [was] . . . inherently impossible," in view of the expanionist aims of Soviet policy."[2]

To the extent that American foreign policy by 1945 had come to be predicated on the eventual withering away of Communist power, that policy had become irrational on its own terms. The policy of counterrevolutionary containment was not so much a policy to contain Communism as a policy to destroy it, to bring about either its "break-up" or its "gradual mellowing," as George Kennan put it in 1947. Such objectives were

[2] In support of this contention Schlesinger cites a well-known article by Jacques Duclos (head of the French Communist Party) in the April 1945 issue of *Cahiers du communisme*, which proves, he argues, that Stalin had already abandoned the wartime policy of collaboration with the West and had returned to the traditional Communist policy of world revolution. It is symptomatic of the general failure of orthodox historians to engage the revisionist argument that Duclos' article cropped up in a subsequent article by Schlesinger in *Foreign Affairs* (Autumn 1967) where it was once again cited as evidence of a "new Moscow line" without any reference to the intervening objections raised by Alperovitz (see Appendix to this volume).

Gabriel Kolko writes (*The Politics of War*, Ch. 17), ". . . Duclos was the prime implementor of the conservative strategy that Thorez propounded and Moscow unquestionably authorized as well. It fully revealed the very modest ambitions the [French Communist] party had set before itself. And in responding critically to it the American government and those who later shared its premises revealed that what disturbed them was not the practice Duclos advocated, but the more significant fact that they considered the mere existence of a powerful Communist party, on any terms, as a threat to United States interests. For Duclos made one critical point: the Communists would pursue a moderate line, but they would not dissolve themselves, and for hostile observers, implicitly, their sheer size and potential power might later lead them to consider new options more threatening to the constituted order."

chimerical and doomed from the beginning to certain defeat. That did not mean, however, that the policy of global interventionism would be easy to abandon once its irrational features were clearly perceived and its disastrous consequences, both at home and abroad, made themselves felt. The failure of American policy in Vietnam has now made those consequences a subject of public debate. But, in the meantime, the policy of interventionism has acquired a momentum of its own, not only ideological but institutional as well: persisted in over a period of twenty-five years, it has served to justify the creation of a vast arsenal of destruction which in turn serves to justify the foreign policy that called it into being, even when that policy has become obsolescent. It may be that the diplomatic needs of American capitalism—that is, the needs of the great corporations—would best be served by a *détente* with the Soviet Union, a withdrawal not only from South Vietnam but from all of Southeast Asia (and from Africa and the Middle East as well), and a division of the world into spheres of influence, in which the Western Hemisphere would be informally assigned to the United States on condition that she keep her meddling elsewhere to a minimum.

Since, however, this policy would lead to a reduction in arms expenditures, the dismantling of the machinery of nuclear deterrence, and a global arms accord, it threatens the growth of the military establishment, which in turn plays a major role in sustaining a corporate economy geared to the production of waste. Even if it is no longer necessary, from a strictly economic or strategic point of view, that the United States maintain a world-wide colonial empire, it is probably necessary for military spending not only to be sustained at its present levels but to grow; so, that for reasons having little to do with the immediate requirements of diplomacy, the United States may find itself hopelessly locked into an archaic policy of "containment."

Even if the United States does embark on a strategic retreat, "disengagement" may be achieved at the price of repression at home. As Alperovitz notes at the end of his essay on the Cold War and the revolutions, "we are entering a long and difficult period of American history, a period of fundamental re-examination." It is surely important, as he says, "that the process is *en train.*" It is equally important to realize that the process of re-examination will not necessarily lead to conclusions favorable to the democratization of American society. It may lead instead to a policy of what George Kennan calls *"dirigisme."* Himself one of the authors of the containment policy, Kennan since the middle fifties has advocated disengagement. Increasingly alarmed at the breakdown of order within the United States itself, he now realizes that disengagement—"a very considerable retraction of external involvement" —cannot be achieved without fundamental changes at home. In a speech to the International Association for Cultural Freedom (Princeton, December 2, 1968), he spells out the kind of changes he has in mind: ". . . a major shift—a governmentally-contrived and enforced shift—from the private automobile and the airplane" to other forms of transportation; the outlawing of strikes by public servants in cases where "the public cannot help becoming the leading victim"; the assertion of public control over the mass media; in short "a drastic stiffening of public authority—the imposition of some sort of public discipline in areas of our life to which such discipline has never before been applied."

As so often in the past, Kennan has boldly raised issues others are unwilling to face. How many public

spokesmen even understand the central importance of
the automobile industry in destroying American cities,
much less the importance of inhibiting its irrational expansion? Nevertheless the demand for "discipline,"
coupled with the demand for the curtailment of strikes
and the enlargement of federal powers, has a dis-
tinctly ominous sound. Even more ominous is the sug-
gestion—which at first appears contradictory—that "a
radical decentralization of public authority" will have
to go hand in hand with a strengthening of federal
power. Coupled with a program for the socialization
of corporate power, decentralization can serve the ends
of human liberation. Coupled with the call for "a general movement of national unity," it can easily become
a program to fragment the black community and to
render it even more dependent than it already is on
the corporations, the foundations, and the federal government. Without a redistribution of economic power,
a redistribution of political power only weakens the
weak while leaving untouched the real source of their
degradation—the vast and uncontrolled power of the
major corporations.

Dirigisme in practice might be hard to distinguish
from the program of the Nixon Administration—"law
and order" with an admixture of "black capitalism."
Pushed to their logical extremes, such programs demand the repression of American youth, the repression
of blacks, and a foreign policy which, even if no longer
capable of policing the world, would always be capable,
through nuclear blackmail, of menacing the peace.
Thus in time the United States, increasingly isolated in
its sterile affluence and its devotion to "order," might
evolve into a kind of super-South Africa, a reactionary,
racist, outlaw power of frightening proportions, armed
with instruments of universal destruction.

Dean Acheson told Congress in 1944 that the American people could either persist in their globalist policy abroad or undertake fundamental changes at home. "If you wish to control the entire trade and income of the United States, which means the life of the people, you could probably fix it so that everything produced here would be consumed here, but that would completely change our Constitution, our relation to property, human liberty, and our very conception of law." Since "nobody contemplates that," he said, it was therefore necessary to "look to other markets and those markets are abroad."

Today it is time to contemplate changes that "nobody" contemplated in 1944. As Alperovitz writes at the end of this book, the full defeat of the interventionist tradition requires a fundamental revision of "the deepest American attitudes and institutional patterns." Recognizing this, he proposes to devote his future work to questions of domestic policy, and to efforts to change our domestic institutions.

It is hardly necessary to add that the changes Alperovitz hopes to see do not point to *dirigisme*—the tightly controlled and disciplined society which Acheson held up as a horrible example, a form of which is now advocated by George Kennan. They point to socialism— a humane, democratic, and decentralized socialism based not on imported ideologies and examples but on the real needs and wishes of the American people.[3]

[3] Parts of this introduction originally appeared in *The New York Times Magazine*, January 14, 1968, under the title "The Cold War, Revisited and Re-Visioned."

III. DICKERING WITH THE NAZIS[*]

*An essay on "The Secret Surrender" by Allen
W. Dulles. New York: Harper & Row, 1965.*

John F. Kennedy concluded after the Bay of Pigs that
the reappointment of Allen Dulles as director of the
CIA had been a mistake. We are told, however, that
he still could not understand how a man so intelligent
and so experienced could be so wrong.[1] Dulles' account
of his part in arranging the surrender of German armies
in Italy sixteen years earlier offers important clues; it
also illuminates the way in which Dulles helped set in
motion the events that we know as the Cold War.

This was not his intent, of course. Dulles was wartime OSS chief in Switzerland. During March and April
1945 a leading Nazi in Italy, SS General and *Obergruppenführer* Karl Wolff, got in touch with him. Dulles'

---

[*] Published originally under the title "The Double
Dealer," and before the death of Allen Dulles in February,
1969.
[1] Arthur M. Schlesinger, Jr., *A Thousand Days* (Boston:
Houghton Mifflin, 1965) pp. 276, 290.

book is a detailed account of how this "contact" was used to facilitate the surrender of German forces in Italy a few days before V-E Day. The publisher promises the book will convey "the breathless excitement of a fictional thriller." However, it contains no sex and little sadism (only an occasional episode in the woods at a Swiss villa). There is excitement in this tale, but to sense it one must know a good deal more than Dulles tells about its bearing on the great issue of 1945: whether the World War II alliance could be followed by peaceful relations among the Great Powers.

Hitler was sure it could not, and, of course, in the end he was right. Convinced that disputes between the Allies could save the Third Reich, he and his subordinates tried to foment trouble during the last months of the war. His underlings maneuvered both to curry personal favor with the Americans and British and to save Germany from the Russians. Wolff made his approaches to Dulles in Switzerland. Wolff's SS boss, Himmler, suggested a deal to Count Bernadotte: "In order to save as great a part of Germany as possible from a Russian invasion I am willing to capitulate on the Western Front in order to enable the Western Allies to advance rapidly toward the east." This bait was offered all over Europe; the trouble, of course, lay in the hook, and Dulles knew it: "It would have been a simple matter for the Germans to let word leak to the Russians that some secret negotiations were going on . . . that the Allies were running out on them."

It was, as Dulles knew, a "real danger." Yet it was a risk he was willing to take; he begged Washington to let nothing interfere with his efforts to produce the surrender of a million men. Washington was dubious: the Germans had been ordered to fight to the last man.

Talk of surrender was high treason, and Hitler was hanging generals on the slightest evidence of insubordination. The only result of bargaining talks would be to arouse Soviet suspicions. So Dulles' first request for permission to open a channel to the Germans was refused.

Dulles was not put off. More to the point, his chief "unofficial" assistant in such matters, a naturalized citizen of German origin, was "not the kind of man to give up easily." Dulles trusted Gero von S. Gaevernitz, and he especially trusted Gaevernitz's judgment of the Nazis. Gaevernitz (who did much of the work on Dulles' book) seems to have made the most of his favored position to urge the wisdom of dealing with Wolff. An alibi was soon devised to cover Dulles in Washington. He would be able to say that he was "only trying to arrange a prisoner exchange"; and Gaevernitz and Dulles tentatively opened communications with Wolff.

Dulles chose an inopportune moment, for the Nazi interest in these talks seemed to confirm known Nazi designs at the time: American and British armies were racing into Germany from the west while the best units Hitler could muster were being deployed against the Red Army to the east. Hitler's tactics added meaning to Churchill's warning that "the Russians may have a legitimate fear of our doing a deal in the West to hold them back in the East." (Probably Churchill's main aim was to avoid giving Stalin an excuse for making separate surrender deals elsewhere in Europe.) As Dulles' communications with Wolff went forward, the Prime Minister felt that in order to eliminate Soviet suspicions, the Russians would have to be allowed to participate.

On March 8, 1945, Dulles met with Wolff. The Russians, however, were not invited, and all hell broke loose. Ambassador Harriman was treated to a blast of

Molotov's temper: "The Soviet Government sees not a misunderstanding, but something worse. . . ." Stalin cabled directly to Roosevelt that, on the basis of these talks, the Germans were moving three divisions from Northern Italy to the Soviet Front! Roosevelt replied that Dulles was merely opening a channel of communications; if and when surrender discussions took place, the Soviet Union would be represented. Now the Russians were incredulous. Stalin replied that his advisers were certain surrender talks had taken place; they believed these had already produced an agreement "to open the front to the Anglo-American troops and let them move east."

We do not know, specifically, whether the Nazis used Dulles' talks to divert troops to the east or to divide the Allies by spreading this fear; nor does Dulles enlighten us much on either point. He admits that Wolff spent two suspicious periods with Hitler and Himmler in Berlin during the course of the talks, but for the most part Dulles is content to take Wolff's word that he was acting in good faith. That the talks had the profoundly grave effect Hitler desired is, however, now beyond doubt. Their effect was made far more serious at precisely this time by British tactics on the Polish issue. Quite unlike Churchill's approach to surrender talks, in this case the British were so violently anti-Soviet that Roosevelt felt London was "perfectly willing for the United States to have a war with Russia at any time and . . . to follow the British program would be to proceed to that end."

Dulles doesn't tell us much about this either, but it is not too much to say that the suspicions arising from these events in early 1945 set in motion the first important hostilities of the Cold War:[2] Stalin raised major doubts that the Big Three would be transformed into a postwar organization by announcing that Molotov would not come to the April 25, 1945, San Francisco U.N. Charter-writing Conference. Historians have generally attributed Stalin's displeasure to the fact that the Soviet-sponsored Government of Poland had not been invited to the conference, but Dulles' book provides evidence that far more fundamental suspicions were involved. Stalin's cables amounted to an open accusation of betrayal by Roosevelt. In Washington, counterfears and counteraccusations erupted. Roosevelt's responding cable was strong: *"I am certain that there were no negotiations . . . at any time. . . .* Frankly, I cannot avoid a feeling of bitter resentment toward your informers, whoever they are, for such vile representations of my actions or those of my trusted subordinates."

It is a commonplace today that CIA maneuvering often gives substance to Moscow's worst fears about American policy. *The Secret Surrender* shows that this destructive tradition began with the CIA's wartime predecessor, the OSS. The book gives substance to Stalin's charge in 1945 that what can only be called surrender talks were held; and it shows that the solemn pledges Roosevelt offered at the time were false. Whether the President was aware of what was going on we do not know. But we do know now that the talks Roosevelt disavowed nevertheless took place. Dulles' book presents us with facts showing how ridiculous was the American claim that negotiations with the Nazis would not involve the issue of surrender.

[2] See Appendix I of my *Atomic Diplomacy: Hiroshima and Potsdam* (New York: Simon and Schuster, 1965) for details of the events described here and in the remainder of this essay.

Indeed it was impossible to avoid the issue. That was why such high-ranking men as generals Lemnitzer and Airey of the Allied Command came to Switzerland to meet *Obergruppenführer* Wolff. (And why, of course, Stalin wanted to send his own generals.) On March 9 things had progressed so far that Dulles felt emissaries might meet to sign an agreement "within days." Dulles reports exchanges on a variety of points related to surrender. He even tells us how his man Gaevernitz personally raised the broader question of surrender of the entire Western Front. And he describes communications with the Nazis involving proposals to maintain "a modest contingent" of forces in German military hands as an "instrument of order" for the postwar period. Dulles writes that when Lemnitzer and Airey met Wolff, "We all realized that this was a major decision. . . . It was the first occasion during the entire war when high-ranking Allied officers and a German general had met on neutral soil to discuss a German surrender. . . ."

Not much came of all this, but Stalin, we must belatedly admit, was right in urging Roosevelt to accept Soviet representatives at the talks in order to preclude suspicions. Some admitted as much in 1945. By early April, Field Marshal Alexander realized that the Germans were probably using the talks to drive a wedge between the Allies. Finally, at the end of April, Washington also came to its senses and categorically ordered Dulles to break off all contacts with the Germans. Moscow was informed that Soviet representatives were invited to the next round of talks in Italy.

In retrospect it is obvious that there had been little real possibility of surrender in Italy as long as Hitler lived. This fundamental judgment had been made correctly by many at the time. But Dulles has not as yet shown he understands it, though even he is forced lamely to admit it was only Hitler's death on April 30 that permitted the surrender to take place.

What had been gained by two months of dickering with the Nazis? A mere six days. The fighting in Italy halted on May 2; the total collapse of the Third Reich was recorded on the evening of May 7–8. What had been lost? It is impossible to know precisely, but insofar as the possibility of peace depended on trust and mutual confidence, that possibility had been damaged. *The Secret Surrender* reminds us that the Cold War cannot be understood simply as an American response to a Soviet challenge, but rather as the insidious interaction of mutual suspicions, blame for which must be shared by all.

Why had Roosevelt agreed to exclude the Russians? There was little to gain, unless, in fact, a deal detrimental to them was indeed being made. Dulles hints that "the impelling reason" was a desire to use the talks to gain control of Northern Italy and the then vital port of Trieste. Other available evidence suggests that some of the White House staff had this in mind, although it appears the President himself believed the talks involved only preliminary arrangements for future surrender negotiations. Undoubtedly, an over-riding problem was Roosevelt's illness; the main cables, we now know, were not written by the President. But the most important factor, in my judgment, was the behavior of the "trusted subordinates" who, Roosevelt told Stalin, could not be in error about the talks. These were the men who maneuvered the President into the affair. One was Dulles' boss, OSS Chief William Donovan, a man "enthusiastic" about the negotiations. The other was Allen Dulles.

Dulles' actions must be understood, if not condoned, in the light of his conception of patriotism. A footnote in his book describes his respect for the "patriotic insubordination" of Swiss military men willing to break their oaths of office to follow dictates of conscience. Clearly, Dulles would like to think of himself as such a man. He is a patriot, but an insubordinate one, a man willing to withhold information, cut corners, mislead, disobey orders, advocate, and deceive in order to achieve what he personally happens to think best for America. Too strong a statement? Dulles himself tells us that he "limited" his reporting to Washington in order to avoid a high-level decision that he knew would be against his making contact with Wolff; it would "cramp my freedom of action and decision." When one of Wolff's top men met with Dulles' assistant to discuss surrender, Dulles reported only the "bare facts" that the contact had been made. He did not want to "create the impression we were engaged in any kind of high-level negotiations requiring policy decisions. . . ." Still not revealing that surrender had already been discussed, he couched requests for instructions in "very general" and misleading terms so as to obtain permission to continue discussions with the Germans while his superiors remained ignorant of his real intentions.

Dulles also describes how he took it upon himself to decide "it was worth the gamble to see Wolff, in full recognition of the fact that considerable risks were involved." He tells us that, even after receiving direct and categorical orders to break all contact with the Germans immediately, he permitted his chief subordinate to meet with Wolff. How does Dulles explain all this? "An intelligence officer in the field is supposed to keep his home office informed of what he is doing," he admits—

hastening to add, however: "That is quite true, but with some reservations, as he may overdo it. If, for example, he tells too much or asks too often for instructions, he is likely to get some he doesn't relish. . . ." It is not difficult to understand why, in 1961, after Dulles' vague and misleading advocacy of the Bay of Pigs invasion, Kennedy reluctantly concluded he simply could not "estimate his meaning when he tells me things."[3]

Larger questions of statesmanship have always been beyond Dulles. In 1945 he believed so deeply in surrender talks that he was willing to deceive his government to gain time until all would see the opportunities he thought he saw so clearly. Such must have been the patriotic "reservations" that led him to withhold information, disobey orders, and thereby contribute to the disruption of Allied relations. All one can do with untrustworthy subordinates, as Kennedy discovered, is to fire them, as he fired Dulles. But the firing often comes too late: Dulles' secret surrender prefigured such other zealously advocated Cold War intelligence operations as the U-2 incident and the Bay of Pigs invasion. All three served to destroy hopes of cooperation and to poison the international atmosphere. How, asked John Kennedy, could a man so *intelligent* be so wrong? The answer can be found in a view of reality that has characterized the Cold War, a view so certain it can do no wrong that it will surrender both the national interest and simple honesty to its myopic conception of patriotism.

[3] *A Thousand Days,* p. 276.

IV. HOW DID THE COLD WAR BEGIN?

An essay on Beginnings of the Cold War *by Martin F. Herz. Bloomington: Indiana University Press, 1966.*

Writing as "Mr. X," George Kennan suggested twenty years ago that the mechanism of Soviet diplomacy "moves inexorably along the prescribed path, like a persistent toy automobile wound up and headed in a given direction, stopping only when it meets with some unanswerable force."[1] A generation of Americans quickly embraced Kennan's view as an explanation of the tension, danger, and waste of the Cold War. But was his theory of inexorable Soviet expansion—and its matching recommendation of "containment"—correct? A cautious but important book, *Beginnings of the Cold War*, suggests we might well have been more critical of so mechanistic an idea of the way Great Powers act and how the Cold War began.

Martin F. Herz is currently [1966] a United States diplomat serving in Teheran. His book is mainly concerned with the few months between the 1945 Yalta

[1] *Foreign Affairs*, July, 1947.

and Potsdam conferences. It is well documented and contains no polemic; indeed, as he says, "the author expresses few views of his own. . . ." The book begins by recapitulating the main issues in dispute when Truman became President: Poland, German reparations, Lend-Lease aid. It moves from the Polish issue to a broader discussion of spheres of influence, and from reparations and Lend-Lease to a general analysis of aid to Russia and its relation to other diplomatic considerations. The two issues are integrated in a brief concluding discussion of how the "die was cast" in 1945 and the Cold War begun.

Any examination of the very earliest postwar period forces us to think about developments *before* 1947 when it was decided to contain the Soviet Union by "unanswerable force." Herz's study is important because it makes two serious judgments about this period: first, that in 1945 Soviet policy was by no means inexorably prescribed and expansionist; second, that mistakes made by American officials just after the war may well have prevented the kind of compromise and accommodation that is just beginning to emerge in Europe today.

These suggestions recall Walter Lippmann's *The Cold War,* published in 1947, which also argued—with greater candor and less detail—that the Russians might have been willing to accept a negotiated settlement in 1945 and 1946, but that United States policy ignored opportunities to meet them halfway. Lippmann's now little-remembered book offered a powerful critique of Kennan's theory of Soviet expansion and American containment. If Herz's view is correct, accepted interpretations of American Russian relations are called into question. And if Lippmann was right in saying that

American policy helped to prevent an accommodation in 1945 and 1946, the Cold War itself must be regarded, at least in part, as the result of fundamental errors of American diplomacy. These are startling conclusions, but anyone willing to bring an open mind to Herz's book or to Lippmann's will find that they have exposed many weaknesses in the usual explanations of early events in the Cold War.

No one, of course, can be certain of "what might have been." But Herz refutes at least one accepted myth. Contrary to current historical reconstructions, there is abundant evidence that American leaders in 1945 were not much worried about the expansion of Communism into *Western* Europe. That worry came later. In the days just after the war, most Communists in Italy, France, and elsewhere were cooperating with bourgeois governments. At Potsdam, in 1945, Truman regarded the Russians' desires for concessions beyond their area of occupation as largely bluff. The major issues in dispute were all in Eastern Europe, deep within the zone of Soviet military occupation. The real expansion of Soviet power, we are reminded, took place in Poland, Hungary, Bulgaria, Rumania, Czechoslovakia, and the eastern regions of Germany and Austria.

The United States in 1945 wanted Russia to give up the control and influence the Red Army had gained in the battle against Hitler. American demands may have been motivated by an idealistic desire to foster democracy, but Herz's main point is that in countries like Rumania and Bulgaria they were about as realistic as would be Soviet demands for changes in, say, Mexico. Any such parallel has obvious limits, the most significant of which is not that democracy and Communism cannot so easily be compared, but that Eastern Europe is of far greater importance to Soviet security than is

Mexico to American security: from the time of Napo-
leon—and twice in the lifetime of millions of present-day
Russians—bloody invasions have swept through the area
to their "Middle West."

In the early Spring of 1945 negotiations concerning
one border state—Poland—brought the main issue into
the open. At Yalta and immediately thereafter, the
United States had mediated mainly between Stalin and
Churchill on Poland; Roosevelt had warned Churchill
that to make extreme demands would doom the negotiations. A month later, in the faltering last days of
Roosevelt's life, the United States itself adopted a new
tough line, demanding that pro-Western and openly
anti-Russian Polish politicians be given more influence
in negotiations to set up a new government for Poland.
As was predicted, the Russians balked at the idea of
such an expansion of anti-Soviet influence in a country
so important to their security, and the negotiations
ground to a halt.[2] Moreover, at this precise moment,
Russian suspicions about the West deepened with Allen
Dulles' concurrent but unrelated secret negotiations
with Nazi generals in Switzerland.[3] The result was a vio-

[2] The details of this history are often greatly misunder-
stood. Herz also vacillates in describing Roosevelt's Polish
policy. See Appendix I of my *Atomic Diplomacy: Hiroshima and Potsdam* for a discussion of this question. Documentation for other facts and quotations not specifically
given in this review can also be found there.

[3] See the first essay, above. The only important new in-
formation in Cornelius Ryan's popularized history *The Last
Battle* (New York: Simon and Schuster, 1966) suggests that
Stalin was so aroused by Dulles' negotiations (and the
West's blatant denial that they were taking place) that he
suspiciously concluded other Western statements at this time
were also lies. According to Ryan, when Eisenhower informed
Stalin he did not intend to capture Berlin, Stalin thought this

lent quarrel, which shook the entire structure of American-Soviet relations. But this was only the beginning. The demands on the Polish question reflected the ideas of the men who were to surround the new President; led by Joseph Grew and James F. Byrnes, they soon convinced Truman to attempt to make stronger demands elsewhere in Eastern Europe.

For most of the war Roosevelt had been highly ambivalent toward such matters. By late 1944, however, in spite of wavering on the politically sensitive Polish issue in his dying days, Roosevelt concluded it would be a fundamental error to put too much pressure on Russia regarding other regions vital to her security. In September and October 1944, and in early January 1945, he gave form to his conclusion by entering into armistice agreements with Britain and Russia, which gave the Soviet military almost complete control of internal politics in each Eastern European ex-Nazi satellite. It was understood, for instance, that the Soviets would have authority to issue orders to the Rumanian Government, and that, specifically, the Allied Control Commission would be "under the general direction of the Allied (Soviet) High Command acting on behalf of the Allied Powers." The Rumanian accords, and the similar but slightly less severe Bulgarian and Hungarian armistice agreements, served to formalize the famous Churchill-Stalin spheres-of-influence arrangement, which, without Roosevelt's agreement, had previously given the Russians "90 percent" influence in Rumania, "80 percent" influence in Bulgaria, and "75

---

was another Western attempt to deceive him. On this basis he, in turn, lied to Eisenhower, misleading him about the timing of the Red Army's own thrust to take the city.

percent" influence in Hungary, in exchange for "90 percent" British influence in Greece and a "50–50" split of influence in Yugoslavia. The armistice accords were also modeled after a previous understanding that had contained Soviet endorsement of dominant American-British influence in Italy. The Eastern European armistice agreements have been available to the public for years, but have been successfully buried or avoided by most scholars. Herz has exhumed them, and he shows that they contain American endorsement of dominant Soviet influence in the ex-Nazi satellites.

At Yalta, in early February 1945, Roosevelt pasted over these specific texts the vague and idealistic rhetoric of the famous Declaration on Liberated Europe. The President apparently wished to use the declaration mainly to appease certain politically important ethnic groups in America; he devoted only a few minutes to the matter at the Yalta Conference, and the familiar rhetoric promising democracy was almost devoid of practical meaning. For example: Who was to decide in given instances between the American and Soviet definitions of common but vague terms like "democratic"? Much more important, as Herz shows, in the broad language of the declaration, the Allies agreed merely to "consult" about matters within the liberated countries, not to "act," and they authorized consultations only when all parties agreed they were necessary. Thus the United States itself confirmed the Russians' right to refuse to talk about the ex-Nazi satellites. The State Department knew this and, in fact, had tried to insert operative clauses into the declaration. But Roosevelt, having just signed the armistice agreements, rejected this unrealistic proposal. Moreover, when the Soviets, after Yalta, crudely tossed out a Rumanian Government they did not like, the President, though unhappy that he had not been consulted, reaffirmed his basic position by refusing to intervene.

Ironically, Herz's book lends credence to the old Republican charge that Roosevelt accepted a compromise at Yalta that bolstered Stalin's position in Eastern Europe. The charge, while correct in essentials, was silly in assuming that much else, short of war, could have been done while the Red Army occupied the area. The Republican politicians also ignored the fact that at Yalta Roosevelt could not expect a continued American military presence in Europe for very long after the war. This not only deprived him of leverage, it made an accommodation with Russia much more desirable for another reason: Red Army help became essential to guarantee that Germany would not rise from defeat to start yet a third world war. Stalin also needed American help, as he too made clear, to hold down the Germans. Hence, underlying the American-Soviet plans for peace at Yalta was not "faith" but a common interest—the German threat—which had cemented the World War II alliance. From this 1945 perspective the crucial portion of the Yalta agreement was not the Declaration on Liberated Europe, or even the provisions on Poland, but rather the understanding that the United States and Russia (with Britain and France as minor partners) would work together to control Germany. This meant, among other things, joint action to reduce Germany's physical power by extracting reparations from German industry.

Although Herz tends to play down the German issue, he does take up important economic matters that relate to it. He understands that Moscow was in a cruel dilemma, which, had the United States been shrewd enough, might have been resolved to the benefit of both American diplomacy and the economic health of Europe. The Russians were greatly in need of aid for their huge postwar reconstruction program. Importing industrial equipment from Eastern Europe was a possible solution, though a doubtful one, for taking this equipment would inevitably cause political problems. Reparations from Germany were another, but the key industrial sectors were in American hands. Finally, the United States itself was a potential source. Herz argues (as did ambassadors Harriman and Winant at the time) that a United States reconstruction loan for Russia would have been wise; it would have given United States diplomacy strong leverage in a variety of negotiations. (Without other sources of aid to reconstruction, the Russians were inevitably reduced to extracting industrial goods from either Germany or Eastern Europe.) American officials seriously considered such a loan, but, as Herz shows, they did not actively pursue it with the Russians—though one or two crude attempts were made to use a loan as a bludgeon in negotiations. With a future United States troop commitment unlikely, and a large loan ruled out, the United States had no real bargaining power. Hence its attempts at intervention in Eastern Europe amounted to little more than bluster.

The State Department wanted to have it both ways: it wanted to hold the Russians to the vague promises of the Yalta Declaration; it also wanted to avoid the specific texts of the armistice agreements. But the Republicans, and even Secretary Byrnes in his later writings, understood the weakness of this position. The Republicans, for their part, also wanted to have it both ways. They wanted to argue both that Roosevelt gave the Russians all the authority they needed for their actions *and* that the Russians broke their agreements.

The Republican attack on Yalta came late in the Cold War, and was combined with a new demand that the United States "roll back" Soviet influence. Few now realize how unoriginal the demand was, for a "roll back" effort—without its latter-day label—was, in fact, at the center of Harry Truman's first postwar policy. The President, we now know, made this effort in a spurt of confidence derived from the new atomic bomb.[4] But the policy, failed in its continuing attempt to reduce Soviet control by expanding Western influence in Poland. It also failed in its bold follow-up effort to force the Russians to change the Bulgarian and Rumanian governments. Nevertheless, these opening moves of the postwar period helped set the tone of the new Administration's attitude toward Russia. Truman, although publicly proclaiming his adherence to Roosevelt's policy of cooperation, seems to have understood that his approach differed fundamentally from his predecessor's. (In private, as Secretary of State Stettinius has written, he complained that the intervention in Poland rested on rather shaky diplomatic ground.) Indeed, by September 1945, the basic change in United States policy was so clearly defined that, as Secretary of State Byrnes later wrote, the Russian complaint that Roosevelt's policy had been abandoned was "understandable."[5]

What was the result? Like Herz, John Foster Dulles (who assisted Byrnes at the time) also believed that

[4] See next essay.
[5] *Speaking Frankly* (New York: Harper, 1947).

the Cold War began in 1945. Dulles emphasized in his book *War or Peace* (1950) that a new, tough line of United States policy was adopted at this time over dimly remembered issues deep within the Soviet-controlled Balkans. Herz prints almost the full text of the crucial 1945 Hopkins-Stalin talks, which reveal the equally important point that, in Russia, the change in American policy produced what Stalin termed "a certain alarm." A few thoughtful United States officials recognized the significance of these developments. Secretary of War Henry L. Stimson, for example, tried to block the campaign to engage American prestige in Eastern Europe. In White House discussions he argued, first, that the demand for more Western influence in Poland was a mistake: "The Russians perhaps were being more realistic than we were in regard to their own security. . . ." He then tried to cut short efforts to intervene elsewhere, reminding Truman, as Stimson's diary shows, that "we have made up our minds on the broad policy that it was not wise to get into the Balkan mess even if the thing seemed to be disruptive of policies which the State Department thought were wise." Stimson pointed out that "we have taken that policy right from the beginning, Mr. Roosevelt having done it himself or having been a party to it himself."

When Stimson failed in his conservative effort to limit American objectives, the stage was set for one of the great tragedies of the Cold War. As Stimson understood, the Russians—though extremely touchy about the buffer area—were not impossible to deal with. Had their security requirements been met, there is evidence that their domination of Eastern Europe might have been much different from what it turned out to be. Churchill, too, thought the Russians were approachable. Ob-

viously, conditions in Eastern Europe would not meet
Western ideals; but Churchill judged, in late 1944 and
early 1945, that Moscow was convinced it could secure
its objectives much more easily through moderate policies. In Greece at this time, as Churchill was to stress
in *Triumph and Tragedy*, Stalin was "strictly and
faithfully" holding to his agreement *not* to aid the
Greek Communists. Even in much of the border area
the Russians seemed willing to accept substantial capitalism and some form of democracy—with the crucial
proviso that the Eastern European governments had
to be "friendly" to Russia in defense and foreign policies. Finland serves as a rough model of a successful
border state. Here, too, the armistice made the Soviets
supreme, giving them the right to maintain military installations. However, the United States made no independent effort to intervene; Finland maintained a
foreign policy "friendly" to Russia; and the Russians
were—as they still seem to be—prepared to accept a
moderate government.

Although it is often forgotten, a modified application
of the Soviet formula for Finland seemed to be shaping
up elsewhere in 1945 and much of 1946. In Hungary,
Soviet-sponsored free elections routed the Communist
Party in 1945. In Bulgaria, a country with rather weak
democratic traditions, the 1945 elections were complicated by competition for Great Power support among
the various internal factions. Certainly the results were
not perfect, but most Western observers (except the
State Department) felt they should have been accepted. In Austria, the Communists were swamped in
Soviet-run free elections in their zone in 1945, and,
after a hesitant start, a free democratic government
emerged for the entire country. In Czechoslovakia,
from which the Red Army withdrew in December of

1945, democracy was so clearly acceptable to Soviet policy that the United States had little to protest at the time.[6]

Almost all of this was to change, of course. The freedoms in Hungary were to end in 1947. The initial pattern in Czechoslovakia was to be reversed in 1948. But writers who focus only on the brutal period of totalitarian control after 1947 and 1948 often ignore what happened earlier. The few who try to account for the known facts of the 1945–46 interlude usually do so in passing, either to suggest that the democratic governments "must have been" mere smoke screens, formed while Moscow waited for the United States to leave the Continent, or that the Russians "must have been" secretly planning to take full control, but were methodically using the early period to lay groundwork for what came later. (Communists, too, like to ignore the 1945–46 period, for it suggests the possibility that Soviet Russia was interested more in an old-fashioned *modus vivendi* with the capitalists than in spreading World Communism. This was the essence of Tito's bitter complaint that Stalin tried to turn back the Yugoslav revolution.)

The Russians have displayed so much duplicity, brutality, and intransigence that it is easy to imagine the 1945–46 interlude as a mere smoke screen. But they also have a long history of protecting "socialism in one country" in a rather conservative, nationalistic way: the moderation of the 1945–46 interlude can be viewed as

[6] W. H. McNeill's *America, Britain and Russia* (London: Oxford University Press, 1953) provides a good general survey of this period. Note that early in 1946 the Red Army also withdrew from control of two other border areas: Northern Iran and Manchuria.

a logical extension of this tradition. That at least two quite different interpretations of their 1945–46 policy are conceivable is now rarely admitted, and the relative merits of each have not been seriously examined. Herz's study calls for a careful reappraisal of early post-war Soviet objectives.[7]

If the Russians were secretly harboring plans for an ultimate takeover, they certainly were preparing trouble for themselves by sponsoring free politics, pulling out the Red Army (it is not particularly shrewd to have to *re*introduce foreign troops), and ripping up the Red Army's main rail connections across Poland—as they did in the fall of 1945. As well informed an observer as Averell Harriman believed, as he once testified to Congress, that Soviet policy in 1945 was ambivalent, that it could have become either more moderate within a framework of security and understanding with the West, or that it could have become hard-line and totalitarian, within the framework of insecurity and conflict. Harriman, though puzzled by the ultimate Russian decision in favor of the iron-fisted policy, clearly saw that

[7] Today many writers simply take the mechanistic theory of Soviet expansion for granted. An example of what this can lead to is John Toland's *The Last 100 Days* (New York: Random House, 1965), an account of the closing months of World War II which assumes that the Russians were inevitably evil and expansionistic, and that therefore the "good" Germans had to be used to help contain them. Toland dwells on details of the Western Front. He devotes much less attention to the Eastern Front, taking much of his material from German sources. Accordingly, the book popularizes a one-sided caricature of Russians as pillaging sadists and irrepressible rapists. (As for the Germans, it is only the rare Nazi camp guard who is a brutal exception to the rule of "the other guards, who generally treated the prisoners well"!)

Soviet expansion was neither inexorable nor inevitable.

At least one reason for Russia's shift to a tough line may be traced to mistakes made by United States officials. As Stimson argued—and as history later showed—the demand for more influence in Soviet-controlled areas was almost certainly doomed from the start. This basic miscalculation stemmed, finally, from an attempt to overextend *American* diplomatic sway. Lippmann was, I believe, correct in seeing that the other error was the failure of United States policymakers to turn their energies to an early solution of the crucial German problem. Bolstered by the atomic bomb, which eliminated the threat that had been Roosevelt's central concern, American leaders dallied over Germany. Moreover, by refusing to hold to Roosevelt's agreement that a specific target for German reparations would be set (July 1945), by permitting France to hamstring the German Control Commission (fall 1945), and by halting German reparations shipments (spring 1946), United States policy suggested the very prospect Russia feared most: the abandonment of economic and political controls and the possibility that a new and powerful Germany would rise from the ashes of Nazism to become the bastion of Western capitalistic aggression in Europe. The United States had no such aggressive intent. Nonetheless, the United States chose not to negotiate seriously on Germany until a full year and a half after the war's end. Especially after Secretary Byrnes' tough speech in Stuttgart in the fall of 1946, American policy was shortsighted enough to suggest a threat to Russia at the very time it was attempting to weaken Soviet control in the vital area which lay—protectively or threateningly—between German power and the Russian heartland. The Russians, who had no nuclear weapons, were far less casual about the question of security; their grip seemed to tighten in the buffer area month by month, as their worst fears about Germany seemed to come true.

The Russians were not easy to deal with, in Germany or elsewhere. Nevertheless, if the hypothesis suggested by Lippmann's book is correct—and Herz's study indirectly supports it—there are reasons to believe that United States policy itself must share some responsibility for the imposition of totalitarian control in Eastern Europe, and possibly also for the subsequent expanding Communist agitation in Western Europe. The *addition* of increased insecurity to known Soviet fears may explain the rigidity that Soviet leaders displayed in their satellite policy after 1946. The first pattern seemed crudely similar to the Finnish or Austrian models. Would it have been reversed had the United States seriously tried from the first to resolve the European security problem—as Lippmann urged? Soviet actions may have been in part *r*eactions to their judgments of American intentions, which may also help to explain why sustained Communist opposition developed in the West only *after* the clear breakdown of German control arrangements. It was not in 1945, but late in 1946 and in 1947, that the Italian and French Communists began to reverse their initial policy of cooperation with bourgeois governments. Was the changed focus of Communist politics part of the inexorable plan? Or was it primarily a rather shortsighted response to American policy itself?

Once the Communists became active in Western Europe, of course, the United States was faced with quite another set of issues. Disputes with Russia moved out of the border regions. The threat some officials had anticipated while reading Marx and listening to Communist propaganda began to become a political reality.

In 1947 those who proposed a mechanical theory of Soviet expansion had to deal with expanding Communist political activity in the West. And it was in July of that year, precisely two years after Truman faced Stalin in his first Potsdam showdown over Eastern Europe, that Kennan's containment recommendation was publicly offered.

We do not yet have answers to all the questions about postwar American-Russian relations, but we know enough to consider afresh whether either of the Great Powers ever really moved inexorably, like a wound-up toy automobile, as "Mr. X" argued. Herz's sturdy little book suggests they did not, and is at least the beginning of a more subtle explanation of the complex sequence of interacting events that produced the Cold War.

V. THE USE OF THE ATOMIC BOMB[*]

An essay on The Atomic Bomb and the End of World War II *by Herbert Feis. Princeton: Princeton University Press, 1966.*

Herbert Feis, who comes close to being our official national diplomatic historian, has revised *Japan Subdued,* his 1961 study of the decision to drop the atomic bomb. Feis has served as special consultant to three Secretaries of War; he has had privileged access to important sources, such as the private papers of Averell Harriman, and his books often contain vital information not available to most historians. Those familiar with recently declassified materials on the Hiroshima decision, however, will not find much new in *The Atomic Bomb and the End of World War II.* What they will find is a sober but uncertain book by a scholar who has tried to fit new material into old molds, while avoiding serious criticism of the eminent officials he has known.

As early as 1961, Feis concluded, as have most informed observers, that the bombing of Hiroshima was

[*] Published originally under the title "The Trump Card."

by no means essential. He repeats this conclusion in *The Atomic Bomb:*

> There cannot be a well-grounded dissent from the conclusion reached as early as 1945 by members of the US Strategic Bombing Survey ". . . that certainly prior to 31 December 1945 and in all probability prior to 1 November 1945, Japan would have surrendered even if the atomic bombs had not been dropped, even if Russia had not entered the war, and even if no invasion had been planned or contemplated."

His conclusion is almost word for word the same as it was in 1961—but not quite. Then Feis felt there could "hardly be" dissent from the view that the bomb was unnecessary; his shift to the unequivocal "there cannot be" illustrates a slight change of opinion. For the most part, however, this book duplicates the old one, although three chapters contain significant additions dealing with the now well-known fact that, in the decision to use the bomb in 1945, the effect on Russia was an important consideration. Precisely "how important" is the remaining issue.

The common ground of both books is a description of the different courses of action open to the United States as Japanese power crumbled in June and July of 1945—as well as an account of how these courses were viewed from day to day by American leaders. There were many options. The first was a diplomatic one: Since intercepted Japanese cables showed that the Emperor was actively trying to open a negotiating channel through Moscow, it seemed that a minor face-saving change in the unconditional surrender formula could have ended the fighting. The second option was military, but did not involve invasion. The Navy and Air Force felt that a blockade alone, or a blockade combined with conventional bombardment, might have ended the war. The third possibility was to await the Russian declaration of war, which was expected in early August. With Japan tottering, United States Intelligence estimated that the shock of Russia's shift from neutrality to full-scale war might in itself end the war unconditionally. The fourth course was to test the potency of a specific advance warning of Russia's intention to declare war. The fifth was to demonstrate the atomic bomb in an unpopulated area. The sixth was a specific advance warning that an atomic bomb existed and would be used unless Japan surrendered. The seventh was use of the weapon on a major urban center. The eighth was a landing on Japanese soil (*not* a full invasion of Japan, but a shock assault on the island of Kyushu alone). The ninth possibility was a full-scale invasion of the main Japanese home island.

It should be noted that Feis does not dissent in either version from the conclusion that Japan would certainly have surrendered before the end of 1945, and in all probability before November 1945, *without* the atomic bomb, *without* an invasion or even a landing, and *without* a Soviet declaration of war. This is a view now accepted by most experts.

But the dates are crucial, and should be examined carefully. The atomic bombs were used on August 6 and August 9, 1945. As Feis admits, the full invasion of Japan, which might have cost between 500,000 and a million casualties, was not scheduled until the spring of 1946. What was scheduled for November 1945 was a landing on the island of Kyushu, with an estimate of 31,000 initial casualties. Planning for the contingency of a full invasion had to go forward, of course, and statements to the press, both for reasons of morale and to keep pressure on Japan, led the public to expect a long struggle lasting a year and a half. But as we now know, and as Feis affirms, within the United States Government it seemed apparent by July 1945 that other courses of action could have ended the war before the spring of 1946. Thus, at most, the atomic bomb can be credited with having made a landing on Kyushu unnecessary.

The real questions about the bomb—"a cluster of worrisome queries," as Feis puts it—were whether there were ways other than the atomic bomb to end the war before the November landing on Kyushu. In retrospect, there undoubtedly were. The Japanese were so badly defeated, both Feis and the Strategic Bombing Survey conclude, that even without exercising the available options the war could have been ended, as the Bombing Survey put it, "in all probability prior to 1 November 1945."

The recent release of 1945 State Department documents shows this conclusion not only seems likely in retrospect, but seemed so *at the time*. The Japanese code had been broken early in the war. Until June 1945 it may have been possible to believe an invasion was inevitable. In the middle of June, however, six members of the Japanese Supreme War Council authorized Foreign Minister Togo to approach the Soviet Union "with a view to terminating the war if possible by September." At this time the emperor himself became personally involved in the effort, and a stream of intercepted messages revealed his urgent efforts to open a negotiating channel through Moscow. During the last days of July, for instance, a message instructed the Japanese ambassador in Tokyo to arrange a Moscow visit for the emperor's personal envoy, Prince Konoye:

> The mission . . . was to ask the Soviet Government to take part in mediation to end the present war and to

transmit the complete Japanese case in this respect. . . .
Prince Konoe [sic] was especially charged by His Majesty
the Emperor to convey to the Soviet Government that it
was exclusively the desire of His Majesty to avoid more
bloodshed. . . .

This message was given directly to President Truman by the Russians. (The President has confirmed
that at the time he also saw it and other key cables in
intercepted form.) Although it was impossible to know
precisely whether the messages meant what they said,
they were significant evidence of the willingness of the
"other side" to negotiate. Furthermore they showed
that although the Japanese sought assurances that "our
form of government" would be preserved, they were
prepared to surrender on the basis of the Atlantic Charter. The "difficult point," as the Japanese foreign minister stated in one intercepted cable, was the "formality
of unconditional surrender."[1]

Feis reports on these messages in both books without
adequately highlighting two crucial facts: President
Truman, as the papers of both Acting Secretary of State
Grew and Secretary of War Stimson show, had told
both men even before the July messages that he had no
serious objection to making the alterations in favor of
the Japanese Imperial "form of government," which the
messages revealed were the only serious obstacle to
surrender. Thus the two governments had by July apparently arrived at a basis for ending the war—and the
President knew it. Feis also fails to stress the fact that
Truman had several months before the proposed landing to find out if the Japanese position was really as
close to his own as the messages suggested. Instead of

[1] For these and other intercepted messages, see Department of State, *Conference of Berlin*, Vols. 1 and 2 (1960).

exploring why the obvious possibilities of this diplomatic option were passed up, Feis emphasizes an issue that is beside the point. Even if the United States had altered the "formula of unconditional surrender," he writes, the change would not have caused the Japanese to surrender before July 1945.

On the vital issue of whether this alteration would have caused a surrender before the relatively small November landing, he is vague; and on the publicly debated issue of whether it would have ended the war before the full invasion (in 1946) he is noncommittal. In one of many strange contradictory asides, however, he does conclude that a surrender might have been arranged. Had the United States made known its willingness to offer assurances to the emperor and had both the United States and the USSR warned that the Soviet Union would enter the war, Feis writes, an "earlier bid for surrender [might well have been] effective."

This is a significant observation, but unfortunately Feis obscures it by quickly adding, "it is improbable that the Soviet Government could have been prevailed on to reveal its intentions. . . ." The comment is odd. The Soviet Union had already given public notice of its intention to terminate its neutrality pact with Japan. Throughout May, June, and July, the United States had no doubt that Russia intended to attack. Japanese Intelligence, as Stalin himself pointed out, could hardly miss the huge Soviet troop shipments to the Far East and the massing of the Red Army across the Manchurian border. In fact, Secretary of State Stettinius suggested at the time that the Russians be included in the warning to Japan, and, until the last minute, the Soviet Union appeared both in the text and as a signatory of the draft of the Potsdam Proclamation, which warned Japan to surrender. At the last minute, the Russians were left out, but it was the United States that decided to omit them.[2]

Even if Feis's view is correct that the Russians may not have joined in a warning—although this is not suggested in the documents of the time—it is irrelevant. Feis stops his line of inquiry just when it gets interesting. By July 1945 there was little doubt within the United States Government that Russia would attack Japan in early or mid-August. If a warning and a modest change in the surrender terms "might well" have ended the war, the Russian declaration of war itself—as United States experts advised—would obviously have been much more potent. Could this declaration have ended the war before the atomic bombs were used? Feis knows of the experts' advice, but does not pursue the issue. Could it have produced surrender before a November landing? Again, Feis is silent. Would it have stopped the fighting before the 1946 invasion? This is not discussed.

Such speculation is not a matter of hindsight alone. The atomic bombs could easily have been held off while other courses were attempted. It was known *at the time* that the Japanese were desperately trying to keep the Russians neutral. United States officials knew that when the Red Army marched across the Manchurian border it would drive home—especially to the Japanese mili-

[2] In deciding against Soviet participation, the United States not only passed up a way to hasten surrender but apparently also helped to prolong the war. Intercepted Japanese cables indicate that the Proclamation issued from the Big Three meeting—but without Stalin's signature—weakened the surrender drive inside the Japanese Government by hinting at the hopeful possibility that Russia might *not* enter the war.

tary—the fact that Japan was defeated. Even without a modification in the surrender terms, the Joint Chiefs believed in early May 1945 that the mere threat of Soviet entry might produce surrender; on May 21, 1945, Secretary Stimson advised of the "profound military effect" of the Soviet declaration; and by early June the War Department Operations Division judged that a Russian declaration of war would produce *unconditional surrender*, either alone or in combination with a landing or "imminent threat of a landing." In mid-June, General Marshall offered this advice directly to the President. By mid-July the Joint Intelligence Committee stated explicitly, "An entry of the Soviet Union into the war would finally convince the Japanese of the inevitability of complete defeat."

Nor is it a matter of hindsight that a change in the surrender terms alone might have produced surrender. Faint Japanese peace feelers appeared as early as September 1944—almost a year before the bombing of Hiroshima. In April 1945 the Joint Staff planners advised that an invasion *"threat* in itself" might bring about *unconditional* surrender. And even before the intercepted July messages indicated that the only difficult point was the "formality" of conditional surrender, Acting Secretary of State Grew, Secretary of the Navy Forrestal, and Secretary of War Stimson all urged the President to modify the surrender terms. Again, the President chose not to test whether, as seemed likely, this would end the war.

Feis discusses other possibilities which recent research has disclosed were offered at the time. Until early April 1945, Russian entry into the war was viewed primarily in military terms—as a way to pin down the Japanese Army in Manchuria; by July, however, Jap-

anese morale had so deteriorated that a Russian declaration was considered useful psychologically—as the
shock which by itself was likely to produce surrender.
Similarly, the atomic bomb at first had also been regarded from the strictly military point of view—to be
used *in conjunction with* an invasion. But, again, Japanese morale had fallen so quickly that the bomb's role
came to be seen as primarily psychological—as a "terrific
shock" which would precipitate surrender *before* an invasion. Feis has shown strong leanings toward other
available "shock options." In 1961 he thought a technical demonstration of the bomb, together with other
measures, might have been tried. Now he "cannot re-
frain from remarking" that little would have been lost
had the United States demonstrated the bomb in an
unpopulated area. (This course was also recommended
at the time by the Franck Committee, by Lewis Strauss,
then Special Assistant to the Secretary of the Navy, and
by Edward Teller.) But, again, Feis does not carry his
point far enough. Instead, he notes that direct bombing
seemed the most likely way to end the war "quickly
and surely" and thus he seems to approve the official
decision against demonstration.

In support of the official decision, Feis notes that the
Interim Committee's Scientific Panel in June 1945 believed that a technical demonstration would not end
the war. Feis also recalls, however, that, according to
the drafter of the panel report, Robert Oppenheimer,
the panel

> didn't know beans about the military situation in Japan.
> We didn't know whether they could be caused to sur-
> render by other means or whether the invasion was really
> inevitable. But in the back of our minds was the notion
> that the invasion was inevitable because we had been told
> that. . . .

What the scientists were told was, of course, not the same as what the highest United States officials knew at the time. And it was certainly different from what these officials knew a month later, in July, when the Japanese messages were pouring in—with three and a half months still remaining to test the consequences of a technical demonstration before the Kyushu landing.[3]

That there was no over-riding need for immediate use of the bomb undoubtedly underlies the one serious doubt Feis raises about the decision. In the earlier book he concluded that on one point the American government could be "fairly criticized": it did not specifically tell the Japanese the nature of the new weapon's destructive power before it was used. This is the sixth of the options I have listed, which was advocated *at the time* by Assistant Secretary of War John McCloy, among others. In the new book, Feis comments that the risk of explicitly informing the Japanese about the atomic bomb "should have been taken . . ." for "we

[3] It is sometimes suggested that there were not enough bombs to try a technical demonstration. This objection, as far as we know, was not urged seriously, if at all, in the discussions of the time. Nor is it likely that it would have been. Three bombs were ready as of early August 1945. One alone would have sufficed for a demonstration, and production was increasing. We do not know how many more bombs were at hand, but the official history of the Atomic Energy Commission shows that expenditures of the Manhattan Project increased substantially after August in the two months remaining before the scheduled landing.

Other objections sometimes suggested are fears that the demonstration bomb might be a "dud" or that American prisoners of war might be brought into a demonstration area if advance notice were given. The Franck Committee and Lewis Strauss believed techniques to obviate the conceivable difficulties might easily have been devised had there been a will to do so; but there was not, and, in fact, the key officials dismissed the idea after only the briefest conversation.

might have been spared the need to introduce atomic weapons into the war." But this remark is made almost casually, and he hastens to add that it probably wouldn't have worked.

There is a strange ambivalence in Feis's work. In 1961 he gave considerable attention to the variety of "shock options" available to the President in 1945. He pointed out that a specific warning about Russia's entry into the war and a change in the surrender terms might have ended the war before November, and that we could also have tried a sequence of "shocks"—a warning containing specific details about the new weapon, *followed by* a demonstration, *followed by* the Russian declaration of war. He then felt it was not only "possible" but "probable" that this sequence would have ended the war "almost as soon as it did." (Had it failed, of course, there would still have been plenty of time to use the bomb.)

Feis does not recall this judgment in his new book, although he notes in passing that advice on other possibilities was available in 1945. Under Secretary of the Navy Ralph Bard suggested a course combining with assurances for the emperor a warning about both the bomb and the entry of the Russians. But Feis does not now stress this fact, nor does he remind us that President Truman must have been able to make his own combinations out of the choices offered him at the time. Indeed, had the President really wished to exhaust all possibilities to save lives, he might have tried an impressive number of combinations of the first six options in the period between the July messages and November, without risking the life of one American serviceman in a landing.

Although Feis understands the possible variations,

and although he knows that there was plenty of time to test them, he fails to explore with any vigor why they were not tested. He allows the major conclusions of the old book to stand. The men who used the atomic bomb were right to do so; they felt that by using the bomb "the agony of the war might be ended most quickly and lives be saved." This seems a strange conclusion in view of Feis's report that other choices were available without a landing.

Feis shows his own doubts, although again in a contradictory way, in his handling of new materials. In the new book he probes a little deeper to look for the initiators of the decision. If it was a matter of over-riding necessity, as some claim, who in the United States Government not only went along with the decision but actively pushed for it? Who insisted that none of the options be tested? Certainly not the Secretary of State, Edward Stettinius. Stettinius urged that the Russians be included in the warning proclamation. The Acting Secretary of State for much of the period, Joseph Grew, urged specific assurances for the emperor. So did Secretary of War Stimson—up to the very last minute before the President issued the Potsdam Proclamation. The Navy Department—both the Secretary and the Under Secretary—either seconded Grew or suggested both a compound warning and a change in the surrender formula.

As for the military, the Air Force, as Feis reports, did not feel that the bomb was vital. Feis cites General Spaatz, Commander of the Strategic Air Force, and General Arnold, Commanding General of the U.S. Army Air Forces. (Elsewhere, General Curtis LeMay is reported to have felt that "even without the atomic bomb and the Russian entry into the war, Japan would have surrendered in two weeks. . . . The atomic bomb had nothing to do with the end of the war.") Feis also acknowledges that Admiral King did not think it essential. The President's Chief of Staff, Admiral Leahy (the McGeorge Bundy of the period), wrote after the war:

> In my opinion the use of this barbarous weapon at Hiroshima and Nagasaki was of no material assistance in our war against Japan. The Japanese were already defeated and ready to surrender.

Thus, of the key diplomatic and military departments involved, all but one can be eliminated as prime movers inflexibly unwilling to test other possibilities. The situation, then, was hardly one in which Cabinet members and Joint Chiefs were lined up, shoulder to shoulder, unanimously demanding that the bomb be used without considering the alternatives. Feis says that the only place in the normal bureaucratic chain where the bomb seemed especially important was the Army. This is emphasized in the new book's conclusion. Strangely, although Feis also made this point in the first book, he did not then stress it. In fact, he even noted that a key Army general—Eisenhower—advised *against* it. Here is Eisenhower's pre-Hiroshima response when Stimson told him that the bomb would be used:

> During his recitation of the relevant facts, I had been conscious of a feeling of depression and so I voiced to him my grave misgivings, first on the basis of my belief that Japan was already defeated and that dropping the bomb was completely unnecessary, and secondly, because I thought that our country should avoid shocking world opinion by the use of a weapon whose employment was, I thought, no longer mandatory as a measure to save American lives.

"It wasn't necessary to hit them with that awful thing," he later recalled. For some reason, Feis leaves the Eisenhower material out of the new book. He notes, however, that the Army general most concerned, Mac-Arthur, was not asked if the bomb was necessary, but was merely informed it would be used. MacArthur later expressed the judgment that the bomb was unnecessary.

The other key Army figure was General Marshall. How strongly did he urge it? Clearly Marshall wished to prevent an invasion if possible. But he was also one of the men who advised the President as early as mid-June that a Russian declaration of war in itself might bring unconditional surrender. At other times, too, he reminded Stimson of the importance of a Russian entry, although he differed as to the timing. Marshall is on record as having favored in May a change in the unconditional surrender formula. He seems to have understood that a Russian declaration combined with a modification of the surrender formula was likely to end the war not only before the invasion itself, but even before the proposed November landing on Kyushu. Marshall hinted as much in the one important interview he gave on this subject before his death: he remarked that the bombs shortened the war only "by months." Where then was the source of the powerful, over-riding military judgment that the bomb simply had to be used, that there was no time to test the options?

The judgment did not come from the normal chain of agency command, nor was it primarily military. Throughout the war the secret Manhattan Project functioned in such a way as to bypass, for the most part, the usual chain of command. In fact, the prime movers were very few. They included Henry L. Stimson, James F. Byrnes, and, of course, the President. Secretary of War Stimson must be included as a member of the inside group, but as his effort to clarify the position of the emperor indicates, he was not the source of overriding haste or inflexibility. Nor, as the failure of his effort shows, did he have central influence with the President. The key Presidential adviser was not Stimson, but Byrnes, the man Truman picked, immediately after taking office, to succeed Stettinius as Secretary of State. Although Byrnes was not formally sworn in until early July 1945, from the beginning of May he served as the President's personal representative on the Interim Committee and was Truman's closest confidant on the role of the new weapon.

It is important to recognize that the obvious pressures to end the war and, at the same time, to avoid any act which might later be subjected to political criticism did *not* prevent most key officials from advocating a variety of measures, as is sometimes held. Nor did "the momentum of events" inhibit the serious presentation of different opinions.

However, Secretary Byrnes and President Truman wished to end the war not just before the November landing, but *immediately*. They really were, as Feis observes, "in a hurry." Why such haste with so much time available before a landing? The use of the bomb, of course, might have made concessions to the emperor unnecessary; but few have seriously argued that atomic bombs were used merely to protect the sanctity of the unconditional surrender formula—a matter which the President had already said was not a major issue—and which after Hiroshima did not prove to be. The only other important reason for wanting an immediate surrender—as distinct from one within the period between July and November—was that the Russians were expected to declare war in early August, and an *immediate* surrender might have ended the war without their entry. P. M. S. Blackett, the British Nobel Prize winning physicist, pointed this out twenty years ago. Since then, Secretary Byrnes has repeatedly and openly confirmed that in July 1945, after the successful Alamogordo test, he hoped to end the war before Russia entered and gained control of Manchuria and North China. At Potsdam, Churchill was aware of Byrnes's objective; he told Eden, "It is quite clear that the United States do not at the present time desire Russian participation in the war." Feis cites this statement but chooses not to credit Churchill's observation.[4] He also relegates to an obscure footnote an entry dated July 28, 1945, in Forrestal's diary, in which Forrestal records that Byrnes made no bones about the fact that "he was most anxious to get the Japanese affair over with before the Russians got in. . . ."

Feis tells us that, in a personal interview with him, President Truman did "not recall" this. But in spite of the President's ambiguous comment, it was Byrnes—as Stimson and Grew knew—who was against testing other measures and who stood in the way of any changes in the surrender formula. The release of the full Stimson Diaries[5] and the publication of the official history of the Atomic Energy Commission[6] have made it abundantly clear that the rush in early August—and the unwillingness to wait until November—derived from the *political*

---

[4] However at one point, quite contradictorily, he says "probably so"—a change from his 1961 "maybe so."

[5] Available at the Yale University Library. *On Active Service in Peace and War* (New York: Harper, 1948), the previously published version of the Stimson Diaries omits much significant material on the relationship of the bomb to diplomacy.

[6] Hewlitt and Anderson, *The New World* (Pennsylvania State University Press, 1962).

66

desire to end the war before the Soviets gained control of Manchuria. This motive also helps to explain why such a tremendous effort was made to speed production of the bombs *after* Germany surrendered. And it helps to clarify why Hiroshima was bombed on August 6 (not, for instance, *after* the impact of the August 9 Russian attack on Manchuria could be properly assessed), as well as why the first shock was reinforced by a second bombing immediately at Nagasaki.

Feis expresses a few vague doubts about Nagasaki without examining it in detail. However, he is forced to take into account the mounting evidence showing that another primary consideration in using the bomb—whether in June or November—was that it would powerfully bolster America's position on other political matters contested with Russia. About half of the new material in Feis's key chapters is on this point.[7] He shows that Secretary Stimson advised the President in April 1945 that the demonstration of the new weapon would have a tremendous impact on relations with Russia. Stimson first stressed the importance of the bomb during the tense fight in April 1945 over Poland. That the President expected the bomb to give him leverage in negotiations, Feis writes, helps to explain why he was

[7] The other new information recapitulates the known story of the efforts of Niels Bohr and the American scientists to try to set the framework for international atomic control *before* the bomb was used. These efforts, of course, failed: first, when it was decided not to approach the Russians about control schemes until *after* the bomb was used; second, when it was decided, in any event, to push production and stay ahead; and third, when it was decided not to tell Stalin explicitly about the bomb before it was used. (At Potsdam, Truman told him only that a powerful new weapon had been developed.)

so tough in his famous first meeting with Molotov. Thereafter, Truman postponed his confrontation with Stalin at Potsdam until he had received word from the New Mexico test. (The test took place on July 16, 1945; the Potsdam Conference began July 17, 1945.) Stimson and the President counted on the new power to help in forcing Russia to accept American terms throughout Central and Eastern Europe. (At the same time, as the Stimson Diaries reveal—but Feis does not report—they also calculated that the bomb would help to resolve the Manchurian issue.) In general, Feis's additions show that, by July 1945, diplomatic strategy toward Russia rested on the assumption that the combat demonstration of the new weapon would reinforce United States proposals for a peace settlement around the globe.

In his first book Feis concluded:

> It *may* be also—*but this is only conjecture*—that Churchill and Truman and some of their colleagues conceived that besides bringing the war to a quick end, it would improve the chances of arranging a satisfactory peace. For would not the same dramatic proof of Western power that shocked Japan into surrender impress the Russians also?[8]

Feis has revised this fuzzy wording in the second book:

> It is *likely* that Churchill and *probably* also Truman conceived that besides bringing the war to a quick end it would improve the chances of arranging a satisfactory peace both in Europe and in the Far East. *Stimson and Byrnes certainly had that thought in mind.* For would not the same dramatic proof of Western power that shocked Japan into surrender impress the Russians also?[9]

[8] Italics mine.
[9] Italics mine.

68

But Feis's revised wording still blurs the issue. One must read the documents of the time to understand how intimately the bomb was connected with diplomacy toward Russia. First, here is a diary entry Stimson made after a discussion of United States objectives in Asia almost three months before Hiroshima.

> I thought it was premature to ask those questions; at least we were not yet in a position to answer them. . . . It may be necessary to have it out with Russia on her relations to Manchuria and Port Arthur and various other parts of North China, and also the relations of China to us. Over any such tangled weave of problems ["S 1." i.e., the atomic bomb] secret would be dominant. . . . It seems a terrible thing to gamble with such stakes in diplomacy without your master card in your hand. . . .

Second, another passage from Stimson's diary, written at Potsdam after the President received a report describing the successful atomic test:

> [The Prime Minister] told me . . . "Now I know what happened to Truman yesterday. I couldn't understand it. When he got to the meeting after having read this report he was a changed man. He told the Russians just where they got on and off, and generally bossed the whole meeting. . . ."

Third, Lord Alanbrooke's diary at Potsdam:

> [The Prime Minister] . . . had absorbed all the minor American exaggerations and, as a result, was completely carried away. . . . We now had something in our hands, which would redress the balance with the Russians . . . (pushing out his chin and scowling); now we could say, "If you insist on doing this or that, well. . . ." And then where are the Russians!

Fourth, from Stimson's diary a few weeks after Hiroshima:

69

I took up the question . . . how to handle Russia with the big bomb. I found that Byrnes was very much against any attempt to cooperate with Russia. His mind is full of his problems with the coming meeting of foreign ministers and he looks to having the presence of the bomb in his pocket, so to speak, as a great weapon to get through the thing. . . .

Truman also told Stimson during the Potsdam negotiations that the bomb gave him "an entirely new feeling of confidence," although Feis misses the significance of this comment. Indeed the bomb served to toughen the United States approach to disputed Central and Eastern European issues even before it was actually used. Few recall this murky history, but it can be shown that the President, who had already experienced difficulties in dealing with Russia, by July 1945 had derived sufficient confidence from the new weapon to attempt major reversals in negotiations over Poland, Germany, Hungary, Bulgaria, and Rumania.[10] More important for our purposes, once the bomb had become involved in diplomatic planning, *this fact itself* began to color the approach to its use. To understand the point, the sequence of events in 1945 must be precisely recalled: During *early* 1945; *before* the Japanese began their rather frantic efforts to open negotiations, it was assumed, quite naturally, that the bomb, like any military weapon, would be used to shorten the war. As A. H. Compton recalled, it was a "foregone conclusion that the bomb would be used," and the scientists were asked not *whether* but simply *how* best to use it. Having shared this natural assumption, President Truman

[10] See my *Atomic Diplomacy: Hiroshima and Potsdam,* which also contains citations for facts and quotations presented without specific documentation elsewhere in this essay.

based a new diplomatic strategy on it, deciding in late April 1945 to postpone diplomatic confrontations until the new weapon—"the master card"—had been demonstrated and had strengthened his hand against Russia. But *thereafter*, between mid-June and late July, mounting evidence showed that the Japanese were prepared to stop the war on acceptable terms.

It was in the early period, as Oppenheimer has recalled, that "much of the discussion revolved around the question raised by Secretary Stimson as to whether there was any hope of using the development to get less barbarous relations with Russia." Truman has written that in April Byrnes advised the bomb would permit the United States "to dictate [its] own terms at the end of the war." Inevitably, in May and June the first military assumption became freighted with the greater issue of impressing Russia. "That bomb was developed on time . . ." Vannevar Bush has testified; not only did it produce an immediate surrender, but "it was also delivered on time so that there was no necessity for any concessions to Russia at the end of the war."

Thus it appears that the natural military assumption that the bomb would be used became intermeshed with diplomatic strategy in a way so subtle it was probably not completely understood by the participants themselves. Using the bomb became so deep an assumption that, as Churchill reminds us, "the historical fact remains, and must be judged in the after time, that the decision whether or not to use the atomic bomb . . . *was never even an issue*." After July, when it became apparent the bomb was no longer militarily essential, the evidence shows that, although other choices were offered, Secretary of State Byrnes and President Truman were unable or unwilling to test them—and they never challenged the basic assumption as did some military men (such as Eisenhower) who were not involved in diplomacy. It seems that they were either blind to the implications of the changed military situation, or, more explicitly (as Leo Szilard reported after a conversation in May 1945 with Byrnes), that Byrnes at least *understood* Japan was ready to end the war, but wanted the bomb anyway to make the Russians more "manageable."[11] Either possibility leads to the conclusion that the over-riding reason for the use of the bomb was that (implicitly or explicitly) it was judged necessary to strengthen the United States's hand against Russia.

We do not as yet have all the evidence, but the fundamental question is an extremely subtle one: Why did men whose ultimate motives are not in doubt come to ignore information? Why did they blot out other possibilities? And why did they consciously or unconsciously refuse to consider different approaches? It is not why they cruelly "decided" to destroy large numbers of Japanese civilians, but why they never even thought this was an issue.

Feis undoubtedly pondered this disturbing point when he wrote his first book. At that time, however, he held that it could be "only conjecture" that considerations related to Russia were important. He has been forced to reconsider—not so much by new evidence, for much of what he now cites was available to him in 1961—but by critical scholarship based on the original evidence. He tells us that "the lapse of time has revealed more clearly the significance of the events recounted." Apparently with great reluctance, Feis has

[11] Feis does not cite this evidence. See University of Chicago *Roundtable*, No. 601 (September 25, 1949).

come to realize that "certainly" Byrnes and Stimson and "probably" Truman thought of the bomb as a way to impress Russia. But he does not like to dwell on the matter. "The decision to drop the bombs upon Hiroshima and Nagasaki," he says in summary, "ought not to be censured."

One must sympathize with an author who has been a consultant to three Secretaries of War. One would also like to believe that the sole motive of the eminent men he knew was to save lives. It is not pleasant to think that they were so fascinated by their new "master card" of diplomacy that they scarcely considered the moral implications of their act when they used it.[12] That, however, is precisely what the evidence now available strongly suggests.

[12] Nor is one reassured by the key Presidential adviser's approach to other matters. What we know is only too consistent with the view that James F. Byrnes urged the use of the bomb explicitly to impress the Russians. In 1964, Byrnes's interest in a "tough" foreign policy led him to support the Presidential candidacy of Barry Goldwater. It is often forgotten that twenty years earlier a similar interest made Byrnes one of the most highly placed advocates of a preventive war to bring Russia to terms. Truman's personal representative for atomic matters and his Secretary of State—the forgotten man of Cold War history—almost always urged the hard line: in April 1945, his recommendation that the bomb would permit America "to dictate our own terms"; in May 1945, his view that the bomb would make Russia more "manageable"; in July-August 1945, his hope that it would keep Russia out of Manchuria; his need, in September 1945, to have the weapon "in his pocket" to impress Molotov; his complaint to Forrestal, early in 1947, that the Russians "don't scare"; and finally his demand, in mid-1947, for "measures of the last resort" to force Russia to yield in European negotiations.

VI. THE UNITED STATES,
THE REVOLUTIONS, AND THE COLD WAR:
PERSPECTIVE AND PROSPECT

By now it is a commonplace that America is an anti-revolutionary nation, opposed to leftist regimes around the globe. As Robert Heilbroner has written: "[We] seem to be committed, especially in the underdeveloped areas, to a policy of defeating Communism wherever it is within our military capacity to do so. . . ." Significantly, he adds, ". . . and of repressing movements that *might* become Communist if they were allowed to follow their internal dynamics."[1]

Must this negative, destructive tendency continue? An answer obviously depends on consideration of the prior question: What are the sustaining sources of policy? It also depends on an understanding of the forces which constrain policy; and as we shall see, the Cold War experience has much to teach us about these.

[1] Robert Heilbroner, "Counterrevolutionary America," *Commentary*, April 1967, p. 36. Emphasis added.

75

I

American interventions against revolutions which *might* move left are not easily explained merely as a series of "mistakes," though there have been plenty. Nor as solely the product of machinations by the nation's military bureaucracy. (The role of interested parties is not to be underestimated, but the military, in fact, is often as deeply split prior to interventions as it is superficially united once the flag is committed.) Again, oversimplified theories of economic imperialism (as America's minuscule business stake in Vietnam suggests) often obscure more than they explain. And the issue cannot be narrowed to the foibles of one man—even one man who occupies the Presidency: only the most superficial analysis could hold the war in Vietnam purely Lyndon Johnson's fault.

The most suggestive explanations of our disastrous global stance come, ironically, from recent Presidents of the United States and writers on the radical Left. Recognizing the existence of deeper sources of policy, each of the postwar Presidents clearly understood he did not have a free hand in foreign affairs—from the Presidential perspective, America's relationship to left revolutions often seemed largely predetermined by historical and political conditions a Chief Executive had to accept as "given." Many on the Left, arguing that the overriding structural features of the "system" determine the way individual leaders react to the "choices" offered them, reach for a definition of the same facts. But neither individual Presidents nor the majority of the Left, in my opinion, offers a convincing interpretation of the complex interaction between system and policymaker which has produced the repeated "decisions" which make up America's compulsive stance against world-wide demands for radical change.

To underscore the critical issue: before reality is masked by charges that the rather dull man currently occupying the Presidency is the source of all evil, recall that when John F. Kennedy held that office he often felt largely controlled by historical realities far greater than one man's will—greater than the demands of the CIA, the military establishment or the special interests of the international corporations. Kennedy, in fact, came to feel so constrained by deeper political forces inherent in American society that he sensed whatever policy he chose, he could not easily risk appearing "soft on Communism," . . . not, that is, if he wished to maintain a secure political footing. After the assassination of Trujillo in the Dominican Republic he felt there were "three possibilities in descending order of preference: a decent democratic regime, a continuation of the Trujillo regime, or a Castro regime." He concluded: "We ought to aim at the first, *but we really can't renounce the second until we are sure that we can avoid the third.*"[2]

That a man like Kennedy—despite his idealistic hope for liberal reform (and in part because of it)—came to

[2] Arthur M. Schlesinger, Jr., *A Thousand Days: John F. Kennedy in the White House* (Boston: Houghton Mifflin, 1965), p. 769. Emphasis added.

Similarly, the overwhelming power of the constraints inherent in America's political culture weighed so heavily on the President, according to his brother, that it seemed he would be impeached if he did not risk destroying the entire world during the Cuban missile crisis—even though the tiny Soviet missile emplacements only marginally affected the basic nuclear balance of terror. See *McCall's*, Vol. 96, No. 2, November 1968.

believe he might have no "choice" but to perpetuate Trujillo-type regimes dramatizes America's *systematic* dilemma: despite exceptions to the general rule, policy-makers have so often felt required above all to avoid the third "possibility" that even friends consider the terms "counterrevolutionary" and "reactionary" appropriate descriptions of a policy which sponsors right-wing totalitarian dictatorships around the globe—and sends troops when such governments fail.

That powerful word "might" I have emphasized in Heilbroner's description thus hints at the tragic regularity of a patterned reflex which, despite a patina of reform, seems to govern American leaders in their recurrent confrontations with revolutions abroad and the "system" at home. Hence, we may ask the first question —about the sustaining sources of policy—in a more specific way: How, historically, did the choices and dilemmas come to be structured as we now perceive them? How does a democratic political culture come to organize itself to so force a decision-maker's hand? Posed this way the question involves the historical expansionism of America's capitalist political economy, the institutions at its core, and the traditions—the ideological legacy of history—that permeate American society, entrapping citizen and President alike.

First, a very brief review of some recent facts:

Since the Second World War, the United States has actively intervened to support deeply conservative or reactionary regimes against domestic revolutionaries of the Left in China, Iran, Lebanon, Guatemala, the Dominican Republic—and of course in Cuba, where the United States tried through direct invasion to foment a counterrevolution—in Korea, Laos, Thailand, Vietnam.[3] In these cases the intervention was by the American military or the CIA.

Again, the United States, financing "second best" governments, has regularly used economic aid as a means to prevent or reverse revolution. Sometimes this is to direct these societies into the preferred course of reform and democratic development. When reform of reactionary social orders proves impossible, aid serves merely to support the *status quo*. Thus, the negative, antirevolutionary stance is evident in efforts such as the Alliance for Progress: "We in this hemisphere," as Kennedy put it, "must . . . use every resource at our command to prevent the establishment of another Cuba in this hemisphere."[4] The "for Progress" part of the Alliance has in practice been defined, for the most part, as either progress through free enterprise and minuscule improvements, or the old landlords, the juntas, and no progress at all. The late Senator Dirksen, despite his conservative views, at least recognized this in his widely reported acid comment: "What Alliance? What Progress?" Elsewhere, to choose just two examples, there were loans, initially through the I.M.F., for the generals who overthrew Nkrumah and grants for the perpetrators of the anti-Communist bloodbath in Indonesia.[5]

In the critical case of Vietnam, United States policy has been quite openly to support the "second" possibility Kennedy outlined out of fear of the "third." Indeed, President Kennedy's initial appraisal was that

[3] See Richard Barnet's *Intervention and Revolution* for a useful review of this period.

[4] John F. Kennedy, Address, November 18, 1963.

[5] The annual hearings of the House of Representatives Committee on Appropriations are a good source for information on the amount of, and reasons for, specific aid grants and loans.

Vietnam was under internal radical attack (against a bankrupt dictatorship), *not* the target of an external invasion; the first policy decision—often ignored in subsequent official rhetoric about "external aggression"—was an unvarnished decision to intervene and put down the internal groups. And, though some now argue that it was a "mistake," the decision to commit troops to Vietnam fell wholly within a much older antirevolutionary posture. As Richard Rovere has written, the war in Vietnam is "an application of established policy." An application, he emphasizes, which has "miscarried so dreadfully that we must begin examining not just the case in hand, but the whole works."[6]

Our first question thus forces us back still further. Again a brief review of just a few well-known events helps us consider the deeper continuity of policy. The roots of the problem go back at least seventy years. In the decade preceding the beginning of the twentieth century, for instance, the United States had sent a warship to Brazil during the Civil War of 1893–94, used troops to overturn the Hawaiian revolution of 1893, used them again in the Philippines and Cuba during the revolutions that grew out of decolonization, employed a combination of military and diplomatic pressure to put down the antimissionary rebellions in China in 1894–95, joined the European expeditionary force to end the Boxer Rebellion in 1900. Teddy Roosevelt took Panama and then sent troops to Cuba to handle the 1906 rebellion. Taft sent the Navy to Nicaragua to achieve United States objectives.

The old and continuing assumption that America

[6] Richard Rovere, "Reflections," *The New Yorker*, October 28, 1967, p. 62.

should oppose revolutions has been aptly (but critically) labeled by Richard Barnet "The American Responsibility." The assumption involves far more than what we now term "the third world." Since instability and revolution appear also in advanced nations it is not surprising, for instance, that it can readily be seen at the center of the Peace of Versailles. Stability in Europe was the first objective; its corollary, the halt of leftist revolutions in general. The American delegation to the Peace Conference, historian Arno Mayer has demonstrated, "played a leading role in the formulation and implementation of diplomatically and politically intended economic policies toward [the revolutionary regimes in] Soviet Russia, Bolshevik Hungary, the successor states, and the new regimes in Germany and Austria."[7] These policies, Thorstein Veblen pointed out at the time, bolstered a basic decision to reduce Soviet Russia and contain Bolshevism which "was not written into the text of the Treaty [but] may rather be said to have been the parchment upon which the text was written."[8] Wilson, willing fifty years ago to side with the "second" in order to avoid the "third," opposed the Russian Revolution with economic pressures, non-recognition, and a United States Siberian intervention.

Wilson also sent American military expeditions to Santo Domingo and to Haiti. And after failing to change the course of the Mexican Revolution by economic measures and non-recognition, Wilson—the champion of "international guarantees of the political and economic

[7] Arno J. Mayer, *Politics and Diplomacy of Peacemaking: Containment and Counterrevolution at Versailles 1918–1919* (New York: Knopf, 1967), p. 18.
[8] Quoted in *ibid.*, p. 29.

independence"[9] for all countries—sent troops to Ver
Cruz.

In the postwar years, Wilson and his successors con
tinued to hope for world freedom. They preferred lit
eral capitalism, reform, and democracy; but when th
chips were down, the antirevolutionary policy too
precedence. An expeditionary force of twelve hundre
was on stand-by alert for intervention during the Mex
can upheaval of May 1920. Coolidge occupied Hor
duras in 1924 and again in 1925. In 1927 the Unite
States sent several thousand Marines to Nicaragu
And throughout the twenties, despite Secretary of Stat
Hughes's promise that the United States sought to "es
tablish a *Pax Americana* maintained not by arms bu
by mutual respect," it remained "the policy of this Gov
ernment to make available its friendly assistance to pro
mote stability in those of our sister Republics which ar
especially afflicted with disturbed conditions involvin
their own peace and that of their neighbors. . . ."[1]
Force, or the threat of force, was regularly employe
in Haiti, Nicaragua, Cuba, the Dominican Republic-
to name only a few—throughout these years.[11]

These well-known examples of the use of nake
power by the United States indicate a thread of polic
which reappears in recent American approaches t
Cuba, the Dominican Republic, and Vietnam. The star
antirevolutionary reality of military intervention is, how
ever, usually evidence that attempts to use less volatil

[9] Woodrow Wilson, Address to Congress, January 8, 1918
"The Fourteen Points."
[10] Charles E. Hughes, Address, November 30, 1923.
[11] For a compilation of the extraordinarily large numbe
of pre-World War II interventions, see Congressional Record
June 23, 1969, pp. S6954–58.

-and therefore less obvious—methods have failed. Accordingly, as even such standard histories as Thomas A. Bailey's acknowledge, it is necessary to look behind every military spasm to a series of political and economic maneuvers which have not achieved their purpose.

Most often, in fact, American policy involved no direct troop intervention. The now familiar attempt to undercut left demands by buying token reform to bolster *comprador* governments is a variation of an older principle: that of quietly satisfying *status quo* objectives —whether or not reforms occur—with any method available. And that principle has been successfully applied in practice for much of the century, and especially since the First World War. Secretary of State Knox, for instance, was a master at using financial strategies to control countries like Nicaragua. During the (very) brief period of the Good Neighbor policy in Latin America —roughly 1930 to 1941—the State Department, partly as an attempt to insulate the hemisphere against Axis penetration, explicitly opposed outright military intervention. During the same period, however, the United States also manipulated silver purchase agreements, loans, and—to the extent possible—oil policies in retaliation for Mexican nationalization of American oil interests. The Cuban revolutionary government of Grau San Martín was forced out of power by American non-recognition and economic pressure, paving the way for the Batista regime. Since the second World War the manipulation of aid, loans, and, for instance, sugar quotas, has been a familiar feature of United States strategy.[12]

[12] See Bryce Wood, *The Making of the Good Neighbor Policy* (Washington: Columbia Books, 1960); Thomas A.

In Eastern Europe after the First World War Ameri
can diplomacy accepted reactionary regimes and gav
aid to them and their Western sponsors—on the opera
tive assumption that this would help prevent the sprea
of revolution to Europe. Hoover's role in destroying th
first Hungarian revolution, United States postwar loa
policies, America's support of the *cordon sanitaire*
United States German policy—particularly its financia
strategies under the Dawes and Young plans—in th
twenties (and subsequent acquiescence in the Munic
Agreement) are all best understood in this context. I
was safer to back rightist dictatorships—or to help Brit
ain, France, or Germany do so—in Poland, Estonia, Ru
mania, Hungary, Bulgaria, than to risk leftist regime
which "might become Communist."[13]

In the broadest sense, therefore, it is not the military
intervention, but opposition in principle to instabilit
and revolutions which might go left, that is important
It explains why the pattern of intervention cannot b
viewed merely as a series of haphazard events, or, say
general support for "democracy." If it were only th
latter, one would expect to see the United States inter
vening on the side of leftist revolutions about as often a
on the side of rightists. But unfortunately, the statistica

Bailey, *A Diplomatic History of the American People*
Appleton–Century–Crofts, 1958; and also Robert F. Smith
The United States and Cuba, Bookman Assoc., New York
1960.

[13] At the same time, the United States did not want these
and other parts of the globe—such as China and Manchuri
—to become the exclusive sphere of another capitalist nation,
for this too, as we shall see, ran counter to American policy
objectives. A good place to begin a critical review of pre-
World War II policy is with two essays—by Lloyd Gardner
and Robert F. Smith—in Barton J. Bernstein's *Toward A
New Past*, Vintage, 1967.

pattern is not random. Kennedy's description of how United States leaders preferring democracy and reform regularly end up on the side of the "second" rightist, totalitarian kind of regime out of fear of the "third," illuminates an American tradition.

Few deny the recurrence of overt or covert intervention. The real question involves contending interpretations of why. American Presidents, even when they understand the constraints which tie their hands, fixing them to the assumptions of the traditional policy, usually explain interventions as necessary to sustain world peace and the "free world." (A generation ago they were "making the world safe for democracy.") Many of the Left, on the other hand, explain policy as the natural result of capitalism, an economic system which of necessity irresponsibly and aggressively expands a nation's appetites abroad. In the former view all interventions proceed from American morality (with occasional "mistakes" admitted); in the latter, from the "system" (often, in vulgar Marxism, as if mechanically, from a robot)—with morality and ideology seen as false explanations leaders proclaim to hide their real motives.

Despite the basic disagreements, upon one point there is justified agreement: a policy which reappears so recurrently cannot be derived only from negative principles. American efforts "against" could hardly be sustained unless they represented policies which were also "for" something. Historian William Appleman Williams has offered what I believe to be a more sophisticated and convincing explanation of the positive roots of American policy than either the Presidents or the majority of the New Left—and his work forces us still further back into history.

Williams' analysis begins in the nineteenth century. At that time Americans were quite clear about what they were "for": both the agrarian majority and the leadership of the country, Williams argues, believed in the dictum that the United States would be economically doomed unless it continually expanded its markets. There was little radical or Marxist rhetoric involved; the concept was a straightforward expression of the needs of small farmers and merchants who, under nineteenth-century capitalism, could not survive unless they could find people to buy their products. The urbanization of the country hardly altered the situation; depression was as hard on international corporations, financiers, and ordinary city people as it was on farmers. Depression and economic crisis created a loud demand for new buyers, new consumers, foreign markets, investment outlets.

The late nineteenth century demand affected politicians and Presidents of both parties. So deeply rooted was it in the majority of the population (the farmers), that the idea of a man's freedom (or a nation's) became inextricably tied to the idea of expansion. At first interventions abroad were launched openly to create foreign markets and, later, investment opportunities. United States policy was ironically progressive—in the sense that it opposed *colonial* imperialism, particularly other nations' colonialism—the kind that kept American businessmen out. Although the United States did have several colonies of its own, its main diplomatic goal—the Open Door—demanded that United States trade and businessmen not be excluded.

Increasingly, Williams shows, American policymakers acted on a preference for foreign governments which would help the United States secure its seemingly self-evident economic interest. As, at the beginning of the twentieth century, America consolidated her policy out of the earlier agrarian ideas, and linked these with business views, she made no bones about what she stood for, and this produced a clear sense of what to be against. Just as the United States opposed revolutionary regimes, it also opposed exclusive foreign (capitalist) spheres in China. Neither was conducive to American economic expansion—investment security, market dependability.

Over time, these quite specific policies were transformed from an economic preference into a diplomatic principle, and acting upon it through direct or indirect intervention to make other nations conform to its biases, the United States became a subtly imperialist power. *Not* a colonial power, but what is sometimes called "indirect" or "neo-imperialist"—a nation which, for reasons *it* thought good, tried to shape the future of other nations and thereby establish an "informal," but powerful, empire of client states that were dependent and controllable.

This is not to say that American policy today is a simple extension of Dollar Diplomacy. It unquestionably is illustrated by that tradition; like so many ideas, however, antirevolutionism has transcended its historical roots. A true idealism, partly derived from nineteenth-century Christian missionary influences, came to be intermeshed with simple economic interests. Beyond the argument of self-interest in the early twentieth century, a broader American conviction (we may say "ideology") also developed: that both freedom and world peace depended on an unrestricted international market. So, time and again, for instance, argued Roosevelt's Secretary of State, Cordell Hull. For this reason, when necessary in given instances the *special* interests of individual businessmen were in fact subordinated to the *general* requirements of the broader policy. Truman formulated the view thus: "The objectives of peace and freedom . . . are bound up completely in a third objective—re-establishment of world trade. In fact, the three—peace, freedom, and world trade—are inseparable."[14]

But the free international market—like "the free world" itself—was defined in American terms. World trade was seen to be obstructed by the state control of foreign trade of a socialist government, or the opposition to foreign investment of a revolutionary government, or the unstable market conditions of a revolution (or, for that matter, British Commonwealth trading preferences and British, French, Japanese, and other "spheres," for these too become targets of United States policy).[15] The prevention and containment of leftist revolutions came to be seen as necessary not merely for American economic development, but also for the development of world peace.

But, as the previous reference to America's marginal economic interests in Vietnam indicated—and as the (often) relative marginality of her economic objectives in other nations where she opposes revolution also suggests—even this concept underwent a transformation: rough-hewn ideas of economic expansion and imperialism only help pose the issue of the origin of American policy; they neither explain it, nor give much guidance in analyzing its current forms and dilemmas. In the middle of the twentieth century antirevolutionism—often rhetorically narrowed to the idea of anti-Communism, and called promoting "the free world"—became not merely a diplomatic principle, but a mission—an ideological projection of the American world view itself, the kind of mind-set which, establishing and protect-

[14] Harry S Truman, Address, March 6, 1947.
[15] After World War II, as the United States was forced to side with the weakened European imperialist nations, the emphasis on anti-imperialism was reluctantly muted.

ing "principles," all too readily—and, from a narrow perspective, often understandably—viewed individual events like Vietnam in terms of a falling line of dominoes which could upset the entire fabric of the rest of the informal empire.

It was a mission embraced not merely by John Foster Dulles and Dean Rusk, not merely by the military, not merely by Wall Street and the international corporations, but above all by the great majority of the American people, who imbibe not only State Department propaganda, but the nation's historic ideals, and who define America's political culture: for no matter how the policy began—and first causes are still important—one must also face the fact that now the people and their representatives are the ones who constrain Presidents like Kennedy when reform fails and their softness in pursuit of the mission comes into question.[16] Most of them also seem willing to give substantial support to the current President.

Until recently, few citizens and fewer policymakers questioned the basic dogma. They rarely stopped to think, for instance, that a positive, cooperative approach to the Soviet Revolution in its early days might have moderated its harshness—might, indeed, fifty years ago have helped the Russians achieve a more democratic resolution of the tremendous difficulties facing their war-torn, backward nation in 1917. (Nor do they acknowledge that resentment and distrust are the logical legacy of such events as Wilson's "liberal" intervention in Siberia.) More generally, Americans rarely see leftist revolutions as opportunities for poor people to release themselves from poverty. Instead, they see

[16] See William Appleman Williams, *The Tragedy of American Diplomacy* (New York: Dell, 1962) and *The Roots of the American Empire* (New York, 1969).

them as threats—first to the United States, then to world peace, then to a myth about freedom and democracy. Most sincerely hope that the world will follow the "decent" American, democratic, capitalist pattern—that a "free world" along American lines will be established. But they are often so blinded by their fear—and their idealism—that they cannot imagine ways other than the American to achieve a Good Society. They do not recognize that policy has built up a web of interlocking relationships between American diplomats and international corporations, on the one hand, and large landowners, conservative businessmen, and local politicians, on the other, which in many nations that are subjected to the informal American sway has produced stagnation, misery, economic disruption, and outright dictatorial terror for much of the century. Accordingly, many who oppose *outright* intervention are oblivious to its informal modes; they find it difficult to understand why increasing numbers in Latin America and elsewhere reject the preferred "decent democratic" road of reform when in practice it means largely ignoring or perpetuating or increasing human misery.

Indeed, so deep are the old myths that only a small group of Americans comprehend the need for radical, fundamental, revolutionary change. Smaller numbers still recognize that Open Door investment and trading demands can disrupt a planned economy (or even a developing indigenous capitalist class). Unfortunately, a man like Heilbroner is only one of a tiny handful of recent writers outside the New Left who has faced the fact that "Communism or a radical national collectivism might be the only vehicles for modernization in many key areas of the world. . . ."[17]

[17] Heilbroner, "Counterrevolutionary America," *Commentary,* p. 36.

One source of the general lack of comprehension is confusion over the daily practice of policy. The antirevolutionary stance has been obscured for most people primarily because in time of apparent calm, quite simply, little happens to reveal it to the general public. There is little in one's own experience which forces one to pierce the anticolonial, anti-imperialist rhetoric to the more subtle informal *imperial* practice. And few can follow secret (or even open) diplomatic intrigues in small nations abroad, although American aid, military and economic, and American power, direct and indirect, are regularly and quietly at work to promote the net of relationships which tie American interests to either conservative capitalistic regimes or regimes of the "second" type, despite the professed ideal of reform.

The essence of United States policy has also been obscured by the misleading claims of those who criticize the "evil" men who carry it out. Many American policymakers are, in fact, frequently, idealistic; *ad hominem* criticism—even against Lyndon Johnson or Richard Nixon—clouds more than it reveals. What critics should argue is that the efforts of even the well-intentioned are trapped and shaped by previous American expansion, by her corporation-dominated economy, and by the structure of American society, politics, and tradition, so that policy regularly becomes, in practice, either passively supportive of reaction or, at worst, indiscriminately interventionist against revolution. Men make mistakes deciding issues—but the "system" sets the terms of the issues they decide; and, as we shall ultimately have to conclude, it is the "system" and its traditions which must therefore be challenged.

II

This brief review of some of the sustaining sources of current attitudes permits an approach to our second issue—what the Cold War reveals about the forces which may constrain policy. First it is clear that much of the tactical maneuvering of the Cold War period —which is usually discussed mainly in terms of power politics—when viewed from the vantage point of a longer historical perspective, flows logically from the deeper assumptions. Indeed, the past twenty-five years of American-Soviet relations are greatly illuminated by reference to the older antirevolutionary tradition of opposing challenges by the left.

The 1947 containment doctrine is taken by supporters of postwar American policy as the appropriate point to begin an analysis of the Cold War. New research, however, has shown how deeply in error is the common view that the Cold War began when the Soviet Union tried to take over Western Europe in 1947.[18] Rather, what must be recognized is that *throughout the Second*

[18] A rash of books on United States foreign policy during this period has recently been published. Two are extremely valuable: Walter Lafeber's *America, Russia, and the Cold War, 1945–1966* (New York: John Wiley & Sons, 1967) is the best brief one-volume survey of the postwar period. It is usefully supplemented by Richard Barnet's *Intervention and Revolution: America's Confrontation with Insurgent Movements Around the World* (New York: New American Library, 1968). Despite shortcomings (Lafeber is forced to compress far too much into too short a space; Barnet explicitly ignores much important pre-1945 history), both are excellent, especially for college teaching. David Horowitz's *Containment and Revolution* (Boston: Beacon Press, 1967) is a rather mixed collection of essays, some bad, some brilliant; William Appleman Williams' contribution on American intervention in Russia is a powerful antidote for those

World War United States policy was based on deep-seated and continuing assumptions which opposed fundamental leftward changes in Eastern Europe as they had regularly consistently opposed similar challenges elsewhere. American policy, which had fought the Soviet Revolution in 1917, twenty-eight years later could accept neither the logical border area consequences of the Bolshevik takeover, nor new spontaneous revolutions in Eastern Europe, nor any combination of the two forms of change which ran counter to the traditional American stance.

It is now clear that the *first* policy arena was not Western Europe and the issue not Soviet expansion, at least not in the sense Americans usually think about. There is very little evidence, in fact, that as World War II ended American policymakers even thought seriously about containing the outward military thrust of an aggressive Russia into Western Europe, as they *later* claimed. George F. Kennan has written, "We did not see any appreciable danger . . . of an outright Soviet military attack. We saw no evidence that such an attack entered into the pattern of Soviet outlooks and intentions. We saw very strong evidence that it did not."[19] Averell Harriman, then Ambassador to the Soviet Union, told the Secretary of State's Staff Commit-

---

who think current interventions are somehow aberrant "mistakes" in a tradition of liberal policy; in the Horowitz volume also, Isaac Deutscher's discussion, "Myths of the Cold War," is (as was most of his work) extremely useful. A final book, Louis J. Halle's *The Cold War as History* (New York: Harper & Row, 1967) is a little more than an aloof rehash of official views—plus an expression of the current sophisticate Washington concession that the United States may have made a few mistakes at the beginning of the Cold War, perhaps (!).

[19] George F. Kennan, "The Quest for Concept," *Harvard Today,* Autumn, 1967, p. 15.

tee that "he was . . . not much worried about the Soviet Union's taking the offensive. . . ."[20] And Truman's Secretary of State, James Byrnes, stressed on many occasions that in 1945 and 1946 senior American officials were not primarily concerned about a Soviet military threat to Western Europe.[21] At Potsdam in 1945, Truman regarded the Russians' desire for concessions beyond their area of occupation as largely bluff.

Nor *at this time* were they much worried about a political threat. As we have seen in the second essay in this book, the fact is that until late 1946 and 1947, the Communist parties in France, Italy, and elsewhere in Western Europe participated in bourgeois governments. They were cooperative through much of the period, and when not cooperative, in line with Soviet policy, they confined their role to that of a traditional parliamentary opposition. In France, for instance, the Communists, who were key resistance figures, in a strategically crucial move disarmed themselves. Although they undoubtedly came to regret this decision when they *later* became more militant, they never regained either the prestige of their wartime status or their military power. According to Milovan Djilas, Stalin's approach to the Greek Communists was blunt: " 'The uprising . . . has to fold up.' (He used for this the word '*svernut*,' which means literally *to roll up*.)"[22] Given this policy, the West had relatively little diffi-

---

[20] Minutes of the Secretary of State's Staff Committee, Saturday Morning, April 21, 1945, in *Foreign Relations of the United States: Diplomatic Papers, 1945*, Vol. V, *Europe* (Washington: 1967), p. 844.

[21] See, for example, James F. Byrnes, *Speaking Frankly* (New York: Harper and Brothers, 1947), pp. 294–95.

[22] Milovan Djilas, *Conversations with Stalin* (New York: Harcourt, 1962), p. 181.

culty putting down Communist challenges not only in Greece, but, critically, in France and Italy.[23]

The major issues in dispute at the end of the war did not involve the West but older issues of leftward change —spontaneous or imposed—in the *cordon sanitaire* area of *Eastern* Europe, an area now deep within the 1945 zone of Soviet military occupation. Secretary Byrnes defined major left demands in the area as antagonistic to the United States, and to her traditional interest in market place economic and political freedom. He had no doubt about what his position required: Byrnes's 1945–46 policy aimed at forcing the Russians back, compelling them to yield whatever hopes they had in the border zone, also, if possible, at limiting other forms of radical change in nations not directly controlled by the Soviet army, like Yugoslavia. As late as mid-1947 Byrnes still argued that the United States had the power to force the Russians to "retire in a very decent manner."[24] (Secretary Byrnes, the first real preventive warrior, publicly argued at the time that America—with its nuclear monopoly—should issue an ultimatum over Eastern and Central Europe, and go to war if it was rejected.) In the words of Arthur Schlesinger, Jr.: American policymakers had "rejected the idea of stabilizing the world by division into spheres of influence and insisted on an East European strategy."[25] They did so, quite openly, proclaiming the by now well-accepted logic (we later called it "blind anti-Communism") of opposing leftist regimes almost everywhere.

[23] See Gabriel Kolko's *The Politics of War* (New York: Random House, 1968), for a useful description of these events.

[24] Byrnes, *Speaking Frankly*, p. 295.

[25] Arthur M. Schlesinger, Jr., "Origins of the Cold War," *Foreign Affairs*, October 1967, p. 36.

The continuation of the traditional United States policy was often wrapped in rhetoric which suggested that America's only interest lay in promoting democracy, civil liberties, and free elections around the world. In part, that *was* her interest. In part her policy derived from a true idealism and from horror at some of Stalin's more brutal installations of revolution from above. (And, it must be acknowledged, it was not easy to judge to what extent an overthrow of the old, semifeudal systems of Eastern Europe was the inevitable result of the war, or the calculated work of the Soviet Union.) Even admitting the inevitability of change, the extent of change—and the forms it would take—was clearly debatable.

But as newer documents show in detail, United States policy also contained powerful elements of a very old idea of self-interest—of quite explicit, repeated, and insistent demands for an Open Door for American goods and American investments in accord with the concepts of the informal empire. Since it is hard to see how the *ancien régimes* could have survived on their own, still harder to find much historic or social basis for the judgment that liberal, democratic, capitalistic governments could possibly have been made to work in the war-torn area, America's interests were defined in ways all but deaf to the necessity for change—a necessity which could not be denied—whether Stalin, local revolutionaries, or the United States liked it or not. If, in fact, there was little middle ground possible (as seems clear from almost every country save Czechoslovakia), had the United States achieved its objectives—noble ideals again notwithstanding—there would have followed a return in much of Eastern Europe to the Dark Ages of regimes similar in many respects to those which had controlled the area before the war—to governments, in short, of the "second" type—like the dictatorship America now supports in Greece.

The transformation of the historic assumptions of United States policy into a strategy aimed specifically at preventing leftist control—spontaneous or Soviet imposed—in Eastern Europe is easily documented now that archives for 1945–46 are being opened. It is clear that the United States applied every kind of pressure in the diplomatic arsenal—short of a land invasion—to prevent the institution of left governments. The policy, of course, failed—more accurately, perhaps, it backfired. But the latest volumes of State Department Documents show, for instance, that in April 1945 Harriman suggested that the State Department "get control of all the activities of agencies dealing with the Soviet Union so that pressure can be put on or taken off, as required."[26] In the same way, the Department reduced most dealings with Eastern Europe into an attack on Communist and other groups willing to work with the Soviet Union there.

The United States regularly intervened in internal political matters in Eastern Europe. It attempted to withhold diplomatic recognition until various demands were met; the State Department sent a barrage of protests about particular legislative acts, about election conditions, about trade treaties with the Soviet Union, about press coverage of Truman's speeches, about a New York *Times* correspondent's telegram being held up. In Bulgaria, United States representative Maynard Barnes held "clandestine" meetings (to use his term) with the anti-Communist political leaders. In Poland,

[26] Minutes of the Secretary of State's Staff Committee, April 21, 1945, *Foreign Relations of the United States . . . 1945*, Vol. V, p. 844.

Ambassador Lane, unabashed at his open interventions in domestic politics, usually made policy recommendations only after checking them with the conservative opposition Polish Peasant Party leader: "Unless Mikolajczyk advances good grounds for not taking such action," the State Department's typical instructions to the Polish Ambassador ran, "Dept. feels that you should. . . ."[27] In Rumania, the United States encouraged King Michael and the opposition leaders in their attempts to overturn the Soviet-sponsored Groza Government. (Groza, it should be recalled, was not a Communist, but a conservative landlord who sought a *modus vivendi*.) Byrnes even publicly supported the Rumanian monarchy, and also backed the king in his refusal to deal with the Allied Control Council, in his demand that Groza resign, and in his refusal to sign the decrees of the Groza Government.

It is now beyond question that Truman's famous 1945 Lend-Lease cutoff was made to increase the President's political leverage against the Soviet Union in connection with such issues. A mass of evidence supports the Assistant Chief of the Lend-Lease Program's observation that this "decision was taken deliberately and probably was part of a general squeeze now being put on the U.S.S.R."[28]

United States economic policies toward the rest of Eastern Europe were similarly dictated by the tradi-

[27] The Acting Secretary of State to the Ambassador in Poland (Lane), December 13, 1945, in *Foreign Relations of the United States . . . 1945*, Vol. V, p. 430.

[28] Memorandum by the Assistant Chief of the Division of Lend-Lease and Surplus War Property (Maxwell), August 21, 1945, in *Foreign Relations of the United States . . . 1945*, Vol. V, p. 1033. See also my *Atomic Diplomacy: Hiroshima and Potsdam* (New York, 1965).

tional strategy. Byrnes's handling of credits to Czechoslovakia, for instance, is best described in his own
words. The following episode took place a year and a
half *before* the 1948 Communist coup, unquestionably
a period of democracy in Czechoslovakia. "On one occasion when M. Vyshinski [the Soviet representative]
was repeating the charge that the United States was
trying to dominate the world with 'hand-outs,' I no-
ticed he was heartily applauded at the end of his remarks by two of the Czechoslovakian delegates. [After
investigating Czech relations with Rumania], . . . I immediately cabled instructions to the State Department
to stop the extension of credit to Czechoslovakia. . . .
I told [Jan Masaryk] . . . that there would be an end
to relief appropriations or credits to a government
whose officials could applaud a denunciation of the
United States. . . ."[29]

The United States attached Open Door and most-
favored-nation clauses to Export-Import Bank loans and
war-surplus credits, to the satellite peace treaties and
the International Trade Organization Charter. American disapproval of state-controlled foreign trade and
of bilateral trade agreement was behind most of her
postwar economic strategy. All these mechanisms were
designed to minimize *both* radical change and Russian
influence in Eastern Europe—and to maximize American influence. The maneuverings did not, however, im-
ply a crude, mechanical approach. United States policy, for instance, worked in harmony with Soviet policy
to support Chiang Kai-shek (a fact little recalled by
Americans, but not forgotten by the Chinese Communists). Both the United States and the Soviet Union
acquiesced in British suppression of the indigenous

[29] James F. Byrnes, *Speaking Frankly,* p. 143.

Greek revolution. At a later stage, however, the United States supported Tito against Stalin.

Adding to the complications, there is considerable evidence, such as the Soviet-sponsored free elections in Hungary in 1945, which routed the Communist Party, that the Russians may not have intended total Communist control even in the areas of Eastern Europe occupied by their armies. Both Finland and Austria suggest alternative possibilities. Churchill thought that so long as Russian security objectives were met, the original Soviet intent was also to establish considerable freedom in Poland—and that the original policy was later reversed (for reasons we shall examine below).[30] Poland being the most important test case, it is worth re-emphasizing this point by recalling also that during much of the war Averell Harriman was convinced that the Soviets, for their own reasons, were quite "sincere in their willingness to have a strong and independent Poland emerge providing, of course, that it is well disposed toward the Soviet Union."[31]

In his book *The Politics of War* Gabriel Kolko has examined the complexities of Soviet policy. Noting that Stalin had little regard for (or sympathy with) spontaneous revolutionaries he could not control, Kolko concludes that as the war ended

> . . . the Soviet Union was pursuing a pluralistic policy in Eastern Europe based on the specific political conditions in each country. No single nation, whether Czechoslovakia or Poland, revealed the overall intentions of the Russians,

[30] Sir Llewellyn Woodward, *British Foreign Policy in the Second World War* (London: British Information Services, 1962), p. 500.

[31] Quoted in Kolko, *The Politics of War: The World and U. S. Foreign Policy 1943–1945* (New York: Random House, 1968), p. 112.

nor could anyone say the Russians had embarked on a final course. Yugoslavia exposed its desire to subsume the impulses of the local Communists within its more conservative global and military policies, revealing an inability to impose monolithic discipline on an indigenous, powerful party. Rumania disclosed a Soviet desire to apply an Italian formula to a situation that was as yet uncrystallized, and Finland indicated its willingness to trade neutrality for easy annexation. Czechoslovakia showed the Russians' cordial enthusiasm for a reintegration with the West within a non-Communist framework if nonalignment provided for the ultimate question of military security. And Poland lay bare the fact that the U.S.S.R. would be implacably hostile toward those seeking to reimpose prewar diplomacy on new realities.[32]

But the critical point in all of this relates to *American* policy, not Soviet; and it must not be allowed to disappear in the complicated history, nor in the fact that the switch to subsequent Communist regimes in Eastern Europe was neither democratic nor revolutionary in the traditional sense. We may pause in our review to reflect upon the historical fact that *both* the United States decision to oppose radical governments in Eastern Europe *and* the policy of opposition to the Soviet Union itself can ultimately be explained only by reference to the older, persistent tradition of opposition to revolutions of the left. The mix of ideas which guided men in the mid-twentieth century were the product of a long and continuous historical evolution. They must be understood if we are to comprehend how millions of Americans came so easily after World War II to permit the enormous waste and irrationality of the Cold War. And this requires that we study the forces, economic interests, and strategies which propelled American pol-

[32] *Ibid.*, p. 139.

icy, ultimately, into such dubious posture around the globe. How, over the course of the century, did it come about that Americans—people of a rather insulated continent—came somehow to believe in the early postwar years their vital interests might depend on whether, for example, their government supported or opposed the bankrupt monarchy of Rumania—or, more recently, the military rulers of South Vietnam?

As we ponder such questions it is also important to remember that the purpose of reviewing the Cold War—and of focusing on *American* policies—is not to apportion credit and blame for the dreary history of the last twenty-five years, still less to condone the inhumanities and imperialism of Soviet policy. It is rather to understand how we got to where we now are—and to recall that the issues in dispute between the United States and the Soviet Union at the outset were very traditional ones. They did *not* involve a general threat of Moscow-directed expansion to achieve global revolution. (The Russians were incredibly docile on that issue, as their acceptance of Chiang Kai-shek in China, reaction in Greece, and even the monarchy in Italy revealed.) At issue were very specific and very old questions in Eastern Europe—and the primary policy initiative came from the United States.

As I have tried to show elsewhere, it was an initiative which blindly pressed home historic objectives in an area the Russian people and their leaders associated with two invasions of the homeland, with Nazi concentration camps, and with twenty million Soviet war casualties. As Walter Lippmann repeatedly urged, just after World War II, the Russians had justifiable worries about Eastern Europe—and United States policy only increased their fears by recalling the long history of

American acceptance of the *cordon sanitaire* and her preference for the fascist, anti-Communist regimes of the "second" type during the thirties. Moreover, it was both silly and counterproductive to try to intervene in an area occupied by Russian troops, well beyond the reach of United States power.

Stalin's rather mixed policy in Eastern Europe was abandoned after 1947. Many American writers argue this was inevitable. But it may well be that the reason for the policy reversal was that the United States pressed its own objectives without compromise, making the middle road impossible. Lippmann felt in 1945 that "the best that was possible [was] an accommodation, a *modus vivendi*, a working arrangement, some simple form of cooperation, and that in demanding more than that we have been getting less than that, making the best the enemy of the good."[33] His point was taken to mean there would be no hope of liberal, democratic capitalism, but it applied equally to those who hoped for spontaneous radical change.

In any event, United States arguments for "the best" in Eastern Europe—in favor of democracy and against totalitarianism—have a very hollow historical ring. In Franco's Spain, Metaxas' Greece, Chiang Kai-shek's China, and Batista's dictatorship within the United States sphere—to name only a few—the United States looked the other way at election time, preferring the "second" of military dictatorships to the "third" of left revolutions. (The United States looked the other way again when the Diem dictatorship in 1956 violated the Geneva pledge to have free elections in all Vietnam. In this case, free elections, as Eisenhower wrote, would

[33] Walter Lippmann, *New York Herald Tribune,* International Edition, November 27, 1945.

likely have returned a massive mandate for Ho Chi Minh.) It all depended on whose ox was being gored.

When one recognizes the continuity of policy it is evident that not only America's role in the Cold War demands careful scrutiny, but that the reasons for her entry into both World Wars must also be reconsidered. The painstaking research necessary to reappraise conventional theories is well under way, but not far enough along to establish a consensus on alternative interpretations. Older ideas of how the United States came to involve itself in World War I have, however, been largely discredited, and, for the modern period, suffice it to say that the work of Williams, Lloyd Gardner, Robert F. Smith, Noam Chomsky, D. F. Fleming, A. J. P. Taylor, to say nothing of Charles Beard, Charles Tansill, and Harry Barnes, has shown—at the very least —that it is difficult to construct a thoroughgoing analysis without reference to traditional American interests— from the beginning of the century to the beginning of the Second World War—in her informal empire.[34] The basic issue is how threats to that empire, either by Japanese or, say, German expansion, came to be perceived by American policymakers wedded to a continuation of historic policies; America's pre- and post-World War II interests, for example, were defined in both Eastern Europe and Manchuria in similar ways; and challenges to these defined interests set off cascading repercussions which were the precondition for mili-

[34] See, for instance, Noam Chomsky, *American Power in the New Mandarins* (Pantheon, 1969), for an analysis of American entry into the Second World War in the Pacific, and Robert A. Divine, *Causes and Consequences of World War II* (Chicago, 1969), for a too cautious review of the literature—but a useful bibliography.

tary responses. Again, the question is not "who to blame," but "how the history occurred."

This, however, is neither the time nor the place to attempt an examination of the origins of the Wars. Rather, we must return to the second question posed at the very outset: Do the negative, destructive tendencies of policy have to continue? As I have indicated, the 1945–46 early Cold War application of the traditional policy to the specific Eastern European situation helps us understand not only the continuity of American policy, but also the mechanisms which constrain and ultimately limit that policy: the literal life and death issue of the 1970s.

Some writers have recognized the thrust of policy, but are less clear about the constraints. For instance, Carl Oglesby in a sensitive description writes that the antirevolutionary policy will persist because

> we have a national style, an internalized system of motives and expectations which fundamentally predetermines our response to our opportunities and problems. My argument is that this system today is basically what it has always been. . . . For matters to stand otherwise, the Yankee free-enterpriser would for the first time in his life have to work for his competition. . . . He would have to supplant his money ethic with a social ethic. He would have to change entirely his style of thought and action. In a word, he would have to become a revolutionary socialist whose aim was the destruction of the present American hegemony. I see no reason to suppose that such a metamorphosis is about to transfigure this Yankee.[35]

Oglesby's metaphor, a more thoughtful formulation than the mechanical Marxism of some of the New Lefts,

[35] Carl Oglesby, "Vietnamese Crucible," in Oglesby and Richard Schaull, *Containment and Change* (New York: Macmillan, 1967), pp. 46, 111.

catches much of the historic flavor of American policy; nevertheless, it largely ignores the question of whether the United States has the capacity to persist in the policy it has historically embraced. Britain and France pursued policies of opposing challenges to their Empires with great vigor—until they were *forced* to relent, or at least forced slowly to relinquish their more blatant claims. In the end, despite America's support to help bolster the *status quo,* they simply do not have the power to continue the policy, though they cling to many old illusions and the "neo-imperialist" thrust will persist for a long time. In all probability, for Britain, Suez marked the last significant gasp; for France, Algeria was undoubtedly the turning point. Each was forced to begin an "agonizing reappraisal" by an internal constraint—the unwillingness of a significant percentage of the public to pay the costs of continuing the policy—and by two external constraints: (1) the challenge of the colonial revolutionaries, and (2) the need to choose between conflicting foreign policy objectives.

When America is regarded not as a unique phenomenon in the history of nations, but as an advanced capitalist society similar in many respects to the large European nations, her policy appears in no way unusual —despite the anticolonial rhetoric and the "liberal," informal form it has taken. The question of having power to continue the historic thrust is critical here, too. Considered from this broader perspective, the opening year of the Cold War (1945, not 1947) is illuminating in that it involved three revealing shifts in judgment over the issue—shifts of great relevance to the problems of the late 1960s and early 1970s.

Although from all the evidence Roosevelt sought to continue the liberal antirevolutionary stance throughout World War II to preserve Eastern Europe from radical change or Communist control, by the beginning of 1945 it appears that the President, marking the first shift in his sense of the power realities, began what might be termed a mature rearrangement of American priorities. Shortly after his death, for instance, Secretary of War Stimson recalled to Truman that "we have made up our minds on the broad policy that it was not wise to get into the Balkan mess . . . Mr. Roosevelt having done it himself or having been a party to it himself."[36]

Roosevelt's revised position—which downplayed some traditional anti-left objectives—appeared first (and most tentatively) in his rather arm's-length acquiescence in the Churchill-Stalin spheres-of-influence agreement, an agreement which substantially acknowledged a free hand for the Soviet Union in its area—in exchange for a British free hand in Greece and a "50-50" division of influence in Yugoslavia. The shift was more clearly delineated in his signature of the Eastern European armistices—accords which (with Roosevelt's full awareness) endorsed a Soviet unilateral right of intervention. Though official Washington (and official historians) like to ignore the armistice agreements, they stated specifically that in the East European ex-Nazi satellite nations the Allied Control Commission would be "under the general direction of the Allied (Soviet) High Command acting on behalf of the Allied Powers."[37]

At Yalta, Roosevelt confirmed the policy when he *refused* the pleadings of the State Department (and James Byrnes) for terms which would have made the Yalta Declaration into a concrete agreement to achieve

[36] Henry L. Stimson, Diary, May 10, 1945, unpublished papers at Yale University Library.
[37] This Soviet right was parallel to the right accorded the United States in Italy.

Eastern European democracy, instead of a flimsy statement of generalities. As I have argued in a preceding essay, subsequent official rhetoric notwithstanding, the Declaration, as Roosevelt was emphatically advised, gave no indication, for example, of who was to decide in given instances between American and Soviet definitions of such common but vague terms as "democratic." *It left control of the issue to the previously signed armistice accords.* Much more important, in the broad language of the Declaration, the Allies agreed merely to "consult" about matters within the liberated countries, not to "act," and they authorized consultations *only* when all parties agreed they were necessary. In this way, the United States itself confirmed the Russians' right to refuse to talk about conditions in the border states. (And for this reason, as Secretary Byrnes later virtually admitted, the Soviets had a basis for their claim that much of the talk about breaches of agreement was mere rhetoric.[38]) Thus, when the Soviet authorities, after Yalta, crudely tossed out a Rumanian government they did not like, Roosevelt, though unhappy he had not been consulted, reaffirmed his basic position by refusing to intervene beyond ordering a routine inquiry.

Churchill also came to realize that, given the power realities, the historic policy could not be pressed too far. Rushing to Moscow in late 1944 to conclude the spheres-of-influence deal with Stalin, he explained to Roosevelt: "It seems to me, considering the Russians are about to invade Rumania in great force . . . it would be a good thing to follow the Soviet leadership, considering that neither you nor we have any troops there at all and that they will probably do what

[38] Byrnes, *Speaking Frankly,* p. 34.

they like anyhow."[39] He recalled in his memoirs that at the time he had considered "the arrangements made about the Balkans . . . the best possible."[40]

Roosevelt began to come to an accommodation with the Russians (and the Soviet Revolution), began to phase down the traditional policy, above all, I believe, because he realized he simply did not have any other serious options. His Yalta judgment that the American public would not authorize the troops necessary to enforce American objectives in Eastern Europe was the first crucial consideration. A second constraint, I think, was that Roosevelt could not easily afford to press older objectives which would cost Soviet support for other United States policies. Without the prospect of a large American military force in Europe, Roosevelt judged that Red Army help was essential to guarantee that Germany would not rise from defeat to start yet a Third World War. (And whatever his personal wishes, such a guarantee was a self-evident political necessity in 1945.) Stalin also needed American help, as he too made clear, to hold down the Germans. Although, as we shall see, there are good historical reasons why we tend to forget it, in early 1945, underlying the American-Soviet plans for peace at Yalta was not "faith," but the same common interest—fear of the German threat—that had cemented the World War II alliance. The crucial portion of the Yalta Agreement was the understanding that the United States and Russia (with Britain and France as minor partners) would work together to control Germany.

[39] Winston S. Churchill, *The Second World War*, Vol. VI, *Triumph and Tragedy* (Boston: Houghton Mifflin, 1953), p. 76.
[40] *Ibid.*, p. 238.

Looked at from another angle, Roosevelt *might* have chosen to press the traditional objectives in Eastern Europe, but he would not have had the military power to back them up if at any point his bluff were called. And he would have risked losing Soviet cooperation in Germany.

Such considerations did not evaporate when Roosevelt died. Yet Truman executed a double shift of policy, ultimately deciding to press the old policy full force. How did he overcome these problems?

When approached in power terms, Truman's changes later in 1945 are not difficult to understand: the central difference was the existence of the newly developed atom bomb, which Roosevelt, who died on April 12, 1945, simply could not count on. In April, Truman, too, could only support the old policy with large-scale credits and the fading presence of the American Army in Europe. But we now know he was advised there was much to gain if he temporarily delayed policy initiatives until the atomic bomb had been tested. According to the President, his Secretary of State told him: ". . . the bomb might well put us in a position to dictate our own terms. . . ."[41] Truman (in his first shift) decided to postpone a showdown over Eastern Europe; a decision which inevitably involved a stop-start, fast-moving set of policy changes. As he said on the eve of his first meeting with the Soviet delegation at Potsdam—just before news of the bomb test reached him—"If it explodes, . . . as I think it will, I'll certainly have a hammer on those boys!"[42]

When on July 16, 1945, the bomb test proved far

[41] Harry S Truman, *Memoirs*, Vol. I, *Year of Decisions* (New York: Doubleday, 1955), p. 87.
[42] Jonathan Daniels, *The Man of Independence* (Philadelphia: Lippincott, 1950), p. 266.

more successful than anyone had expected, Truman was in a position quite different than Roosevelt's. By August, as Admiral Leahy has written, ". . . it was no longer a theory. We had the bombs."[43] Truman (in his second shift) spoke out against spheres of influence— and the traditional policy was resumed full force. Churchill's post-atomic appraisal is in revealing contrast to his view of the pre-atomic realities: According to Alanbrooke, he felt ". . . we now had something in our hands which would redress the balance with the Russians."[44]

The bomb removed *both* the internal and external constraints which had begun to limit the historic policy. First, it was now no longer necessary to have more troops in order to implement the policy in Eastern Europe. The bomb itself was presumed to suffice. Congressional opposition simply no longer mattered.[45] Second, as Truman explained to De Gaulle, the bomb meant that *the United States could handle the German problem by itself.* This critical point is ignored by almost all scholars—official, liberal, conservative, and radical; its importance is that it released Truman from the primary external constraint which had dominated Roosevelt's policies. For if a United States nuclear monopoly alone would suffice to keep the Germans in their place, Truman would not have to sacrifice traditional

[43] W. D. Leahy, *I Was There* (New York: McGraw-Hill, 1950), p. 431.

[44] Sir Arthur Bryant, *Triumph in the West, 1943–1946* (London: Collins, 1959), p. 363.

[45] Men like Harriman, however, urged that troops were still necessary, and complained that the Eastern European strategy failed because troops were not authorized by Congress.

policy objectives to the need for Russian help in Germany. The old policy could be reasserted.

Because it no longer seemed necessary to reach a four-power settlement in Germany, inevitably the cornerstone of postwar cooperation between the United States and the Soviet Union was dislodged. Though it is often said that the Soviets blocked agreement over Germany, their serious opposition came later, long after American leaders reversed Roosevelt's commitments in Germany. Indeed, Truman and Byrnes in July of 1945 at Potsdam refused to hold to Roosevelt's agreement that a specific target for German reparations be set; in the fall of 1945 they permitted France to hamstring the German Control Commission; in the spring of 1946 they halted German reparations shipments to the Soviet Union. (The reparations issue, which also involved reducing Germany's economic might, was inseparably involved with "industrial disarmament" and Central European security.[46]) American leaders dallied over German questions—able to play a power-maximizing game because their minimum security needs were now assured. Having the bomb, it no longer seemed necessary to make concessions to the Soviet Union in the bartering over economic and political controls in Germany—or even to maintain careful controls.

It is important to understand that these early changes of policy (in response to changes in power relative to constraints) did not mean that the United States wished to fight the Soviet Union. Quite the contrary: peace, as policymakers defined its requirements, was the goal. Still, American policies suggested the very

[46] See Manuel Gottlieb, *The German Peace Settlement and the Berlin Crisis* (New York: Paine-Whitman, 1960) for an excellent review of these issues.

prospect Russia feared most: the abandonment of economic and political controls and the possibility that a
new and powerful Germany would rise again to become
a major source of Western capitalistic aggression in Europe. American policy was shortsighted enough to construct a potential threat to Russia at the very time it was
attempting to weaken the Soviet position in the vital
area which lay—protectively or threateningly—between
German power and the Russian heartland. The Russians, who had no nuclear weapons, were far less casual
about the question of security; their grip seemed to
tighten in the buffer area month by month as their
worst fears about Germany's future seemed to come
true. American actions also clearly served to re-enforce
those within the Soviet bureaucracy who argued for
expansion for its own sake. In this way both powers
conspired—as much unconsciously as consciously—to
prevent either democracy or independent left changes
in the area.

I have tried to show elsewhere how this interaction
had much to do with the way the Cold War started,[47]
how each toughened its own stand as it read its deepest
fears (and projections of its *own* expansion?) into the
other's moves, but the only real point of investigating
the past is to learn how to deal with the future. Now,
twenty years later, both the Soviet Union and the
United States have thermonuclear weapons. Germany
lies between them—relatively neutralized, not by the
weakening of her industrial base in relation to the
Powers (as projected at Yalta and Potsdam), but, now,
by her lack of nuclear weapons. In the current, much
escalated power situation, the 1945 policy objectives,

[47] See Chapter IV.

ironically, are largely met. The issue of Communist control in Eastern Europe is also settled; and now a *détente,* based, finally, on United States *acceptance* of change, is perhaps possible. (But, as the Czech crisis indicates, this by no means settles other important issues—of, for instance, Soviet policy, or, more critically, spontaneous change and self-determination in the area.[48]) American policymakers, as they consider liberating left tendencies in Czechoslovakia or, previously, Hungary, are also forced to reconsider the old policy because they wish to toy with playing off new revolutions in Eastern Europe against the ossification of an old one in Russia.

The intent of United States policy has not changed; rather, the constraints which inhibit policy have grown. Twenty-five years after the war, American policymakers are slowly coming to understand the limits of their power, just as it appears Roosevelt had begun to understand them shortly before his death and before the atomic bomb. Modern Soviet nuclear strength is one limiting factor, but not the only one. Even Truman understood that the bomb alone did not enable him to intervene successfully in China. He knew he would have to "throw into China unlimited resources and large armies of American soldiers to defeat the Commu-

[48] The various modern disengagement and Central European disarmament schemes are, in some ways, best understood as modern nuclear variations on the older theory of the Yalta-Potsdam agreements. If the *détente* holds—and security is assured—perhaps such schemes may one day open the way for true democracy and self-determination in Central Europe, for only when security is assured—and the paranoia of military bureaucrats thereby curbed—will such obscenities as invasions of Czechoslovakia (by East or West) be ended for good.

nists. . . ."[49] And for Truman the external constraint, forced by the prospect of massive war, and imposed by the revolutionaries, was matched by an internal one. Like Roosevelt before the atomic bomb, Truman judged "the American people would never stand for such an undertaking."[50]

The Korean War also brought the issue of constraints into the open. Although proclaimed only as a decision to "halt aggression," United States participation in the war (whatever its merits or demerits—and there are many unexplained historical details)[51] flowed directly from the historic policy: America's war aim was to prevent the system established in the North from being established in the South, again a policy historically inexplicable without reference to the older tradition. United States leaders also supported a government of the "second" type in the South although they were fully aware that this was a totally bankrupt policy.[52] The consequences dramatized a powerful external con-

[49] Truman, *Memoirs*, Vol. II, *Years of Trial and Hope* (New York: Signet, 1965), p. 82.

[50] *Ibid.*, p. 82.

[51] See I. F. Stone, *The Hidden History of the Korean War* (New York, 1969).

[52] One does not have to admire the regime in the North to accept the point that the United States again felt it had to choose a government of the "second" kind out of fear of the "third" in the South. Truman himself assessed the South Korean regime thus: "From the moment of [Syngman Rhee's] return to Korea in 1945, he attracted to himself men of extreme right-wing attitudes and disagreed sharply with the political leaders of more moderate views, and the withdrawal of military government removed restraints that had prevented arbitrary actions against his opponents. I did not care for the methods used by Rhee's police to break up political meetings and control political enemies. . . ." (*Ibid.*, p. 375)

straint, particularly for the United States military, namely, that indiscriminate continuation of the policy involved huge economic, military, and human costs—irrespective of any other considerations. The war also drove home a second constraint—again, particularly to the military—that the United States could not easily fight on two fronts at once. The central point of General Omar Bradley's famous warning to Congress, that expanding the Korean War "would involve us in the wrong war, at the wrong place, at the wrong time, and with the wrong enemy,"[53] was that the United States *had to choose* between extensive war in Asia and its objectives in Europe; American power was not unlimited. Third, of course, were the domestic constraints: to press the policy as far as MacArthur wanted would have meant all-out war with China. Neither Truman nor the American public were prepared for this, and, indeed, Eisenhower won the 1952 election, at least in part, by successfully exploiting public divisions over the issue. The domestic aftermath of the war, moreover, produced a widespread feeling (which lasted roughly eight years) that there should be "no more Koreas."

Now, during the Vietnam War, such fundamental external and internal constraints are even more clearly illuminated than they were at the outset of the Cold War or during Korea. Increasingly, as the NLF has demonstrated, revolutionaries have the power to force American policymakers to choose between massive war and abandonment of a military and overt policy of opposing revolutions of the left. The need to choose between conflicting objectives is also clear. According to

[53] Hearing Before the Committee on the Armed Services and Committee on Foreign Relations, U.S. Senate, 82 Congress, 1 Session (1951), pp. 729–33.

George Kennan, the war in Vietnam "has represented a grievous disbalance of our world policy. It has riveted an undue amount of our attention and resources to a single secondary theater of world events."[54] While such considerations in no way go to the heart of the policy assumption, they nevertheless help force a reappraisal.[55]

The external constraints are also matched by the internal. Increasingly, the American people are learning to take political action to block the overt antirevolutionary policy. This fact generates forces which permit (or require) even established political figures to take risks: Senator McCarthy's decision to break openly with Administration policy, like the divisions which occurred among British and French leadership groups in the process of retreat from Empire, is likely to appear, in historical retrospect, as only the first of many new splits in American politics. The millions of Americans who consider themselves conservative in the tradition of, say, Robert Taft, or simply conservative in non-political terms, may not easily support a McCarthy when it means loss of face in the midst of a war. Ultimately,

[54] George F. Kennan, "Introducing Eugene McCarthy," *The New York Review of Books*, April 11, 1968.

[55] The limiting tendency of the external constraints is, of course, not an unbroken trend. For instance, the relative *détente* in Europe—particularly after the 1961 Berlin crisis—permitted policymakers to feel they could increase commitments in Asia in general, and in Vietnam in particular. A second countertendency is illustrated by the Cuban missile crisis, which, in proving to some that the Soviets would back down when the going got tough, made the risks of an expanded policy seem less. (Both these points are, of course, only too obvious to the revolutionaries who are on the receiving end of the policy.) Nevertheless, the longer-term trend of the external constraints is clearly in the direction of limiting United States interventionism.

however, they are likely to join future efforts which demand in prudence that no further wasteful commitments be made. Signs of the coming times may well have been Senator Richard Russell's adamant 1967 stand against the Johnson Administration's desire to send three military cargo planes to the Congo (he feared it might be the opening wedge of a larger commitment) —or Senator Mansfield's recent efforts to limit American involvements abroad.[56]

Undoubtedly there will be further interventions; Americans have not yet found ways to end even the Vietnam War. But they toppled Lyndon Johnson, and politicians are becoming aware that should they continue to lead the nation into new follies, their own careers will be threatened. Slow as this process is, it involves perhaps the one sure point that Richard Nixon may ultimately remember about his election victory —or, rather, about the causes of the Johnson-Humphrey defeat. There is a chance that after the war, a "no more Vietnams" policy may be instituted. According to Nelson Rockefeller, "We can make this Vietnam the last Vietnam."[57] If not this Vietnam, then the next . . . or the next . . . or the next. . . .

Reacting dumbly as the external and internal constraints—like the closing jaws of a vise—force decisions is a costly way to achieve awareness, and it does not reach to many basic issues of United States economic interventionism. The policy shift is in fact only in its initial stages, no more. To slow down or halt military or CIA intervention is the first step. Clearly, the second— now in its "tokenism" phase—involves a critique of the industrial-military complex of institutions which—in the

---

[56] *Congressional Record,* July 10, 1967, p. S9240.
[57] Advertisement, *The New York Times,* June 18, 1968.

brief period since the Second World War—has been erected to support the much older policies, and which has taken on a life of its own. The third effort, built on both of these, will have to break the hammerlock of the informal web of economic, political, and other ties to bankrupt ruling groups in underdeveloped nations—for only as these silent and systematic connections are undone can such nations be released from their miserable bondage to the old policy. The last objective is the most difficult: confronting and changing blind but basic "anti-Communist" attitudes that have become part of American political culture over the last seventy years. This, of course, also entails recognition that America's actual dependence on foreign markets, natural resources, and investment outlets, though very real, has been exaggerated by both critics and apologists; while the economic, political, and moral costs of maintaining the informal empire far outweigh the gains—and it entails challenging the very nature of the American corporate economy which continues the notion that the country needs an Open Door for goods and investment abroad.

Even though our reappraisal is in a very early stage, it is immensely important that the process is *en train*—that the message is beginning to get across. Looking well beyond this war and the divisiveness and repression it is bringing, a measured sense of realism may therefore be possible. Over the long span of the next generation of American history—through the coming interregnum of sporadic and increasing repression—those who oppose the policy of antirevolution must press their views with all force, increasing the constraints through confrontation, political organization, and education. Ultimately they must assert democratic control of foreign policy through radically new institutional forms; the United States must be forced to give up the traditional policy entirely.

One day, if we live through the coming period (and a measured sense of perspective suggests we probably will) Americans may come to see left revolutions not as threats, but as the positive expressions of human beings trying to escape from degradation and poverty. When the nation gives up its sad tendency to prefer the total sterility of the Batista-Trujillo-Chiang "second," perhaps we will learn to use America's great power to help ease the revolutionary course up from poverty. Will America be able to work with other Titos? Will the nation come to understand the radical demand for self-determination which is the yearning of revolutions around the globe? Perhaps. Yet even a move in this direction would be a mere beginning.

We are entering a difficult and long period of American history, a period of fundamental re-examination. We shall ultimately have to get to the root of the interventionist tradition—so that the idea of expansion, of intervention—and the idea that "freedom" requires both—no longer weaves comfortably into the basic fabric of our society—so that ordinary people are free to see that their interests are not the same as those of the business and government institutions which now sustain the old ideology. So, indeed, that we can eliminate at the root the situational logic which traps Presidents, whatever their personal views, repeatedly into antirevolutionary decisions. Accordingly, it is not enough to challenge the corporations, the "system," or the American Establishment elites; ways must be found to speak intelligently to the great majority of Americans, and, with patience and commitment to the long haul, to offer a creative alternative to ideas which so many have held for so long.[58]

In short, we must find means—for these and countless other reasons—to restructure fundamentally the deepest American attitudes and institutional patterns at the core of our system of political economy. Thus, in the end we are confronted with the challenge of change at home as well as abroad. And in the American system, that central challenge—to our positive ideals as well as to our negative stance—is as revolutionary as any faced abroad.

[58] See Williams, *The Roots of the American Empire* (New York: Random House, 1969), for an elaboration of this theme. For a different, and in my judgment, more limited conception of the role of the majority, see Kolko, Gabriel, *The Roots of American Foreign Policy* (Boston: Beacon Press, 1969).

VII. APPENDIX: LETTERS

[*Author's Note: This Appendix contains letters, relevant to points taken up in the preceding essays, which appeared in the* New York Review of Books—*with the exception of one important one, for which permission to reprint was not granted.*]

Beginning the Cold War

I was fascinated by Mr. Gar Alperovitz's review of Allen Dulles' *The Secret Surrender*. I am not competent to judge whether or not Mr. Dulles' somewhat meaningless negotiations helped spark off the Cold War, but I would like to bring to your attention a number of rather disturbing—indeed shocking—statements that Mr. Dulles makes about some of his German co-conspirators. Throughout the book he suggests that SS *Standartenführer* Eugen Dollmann, Himmler's representative in Rome, and SS *Obergruppenführer* Karl Wolff, the high SS and police leader of Northern Italy, were somehow *atypical* Nazis—reasonable fellows, "good" Germans, at odds with such fanatics as Kaltenbrunner.

This is monstrously false. Mr. Dulles, for example, writes of Dollmann: "Of quite a different cut among the German SS in Italy was Colonel Eugen Dollmann." He goes on to describe him as an art historian, a writer, a man who never attended the SS training schools and seldom wore the SS uniform. He neglects to make it clear that the art historian was the official representative in Rome of the RSHA, the over-all police and Gestapo agency of the SS, and that in 1943 he complained to a fellow German bureaucrat that the Italian armed forces were "still shot through with full Jews and countless half-Jews."

The case of Karl Wolff is far worse. Dulles tells us that Wolff "was not concerned with the organization and administration of the SS itself" and that he was "not primarily either a commander of troops or a police official." He goes on to suggest that Wolff was such a reasonable fellow that "he was naturally resented by the more typical Nazi and SS types." This is either deliberate evasion or pure ignorance (which I find hard to accept in the former director of the CIA). Wolff, as Himmler's Chief of Personal Staff, was privy to every act of the SS. To give one example, it was Wolff who informed Himmler of the *Kristallnacht*, in November of 1938, and who sent the SS into action—an action in which 20,000 Jews were rounded up and sent to concentration camps.

The most monstrous and unforgivable evasion in Dulles' book is on page 253, when he discusses the charges raised against Wolff after the war. Dulles says: "There was also one piece of documentary evidence. In 1942 Wolff had put his signature to a paper which requested additional freight cars . . . for use in Poland. It seemed that there was evidence that the cars were for transporting Jews. . . ."

I think your readers might be interested to know the text of that document—one that paints Wolff in a rather different light from that of the reasonable fellow whose relations to Mr. Dulles were so cordial:

Dear Party Member Ganzenmueller:

For your letter of July 28th, 1942, I thank you—also in the name of the Reichsfuehrer SS—sincerely. With particular joy I noted your assurance that for two weeks now a train has been carrying, every day, 5000 members of the Chosen People to Treblinka, so that we are now in a position to carry through this "population movement." I, for my part, have contacted the participating agencies to assure the implementation of the process without friction. I thank you again for your efforts in this matter and, at the same time, I would be grateful if you would give to these things your continued personal attention. With best regards and Heil Hitler!

Your Devoted
W

I am indebted to Raul Hilberg's monumental *The Destruction of the European Jews* for this letter, which makes me rather doubt Allen Dulles' claim that Wolff frequently lent a helping hand to the persecuted in private. Maybe he did—Eichmann made the same claim, after all—but the fact remains that Mr. Dulles is deliberately whitewashing an odious and repugnant satrap of the Third Reich—all the more odious because he was not a brute, like Hoess, nor a nonentity, like Eichmann, but an intelligent and educated man.

Are we really to believe that Mr. Dulles remains ignorant to this day of the nature of his co-conspirators? Are we to assume that he is merely naïve? Or must we conclude that a career that has been marked by a compulsive refusal to admit the truth, as in those pointless negotiations that brought about a surrender only a few days before the German collapse, against the order of his own government and at the risk of offending the Russians, has made Mr. Dulles believe that he can hide *anything*. Alas, in the case of Karl Wolff, as in the case

of the U-2, the evidence is there for all to see. Not
even Mr. Dulles' coy evasions can hide the nasty truth
about "the diplomat and political adviser" who took
such an active and personal interest in the little matter of the Jews who were to be sent to Treblinka to be
gassed.

Michael V. Korda

New York City

The question of when and to whom to assign the initia-
tion of the Cold War was tackled in "Letters" by Arthur Schlesinger, Jr., and Gar Alperovitz, the reviewer
of *The Secret Surrender*, whom Mr. Schlesinger engaged in debate. Schlesinger employs Jacques Duclos'
April 1945 article in *Cahiers du Communisme* to demonstrate to Alperovitz that the Cold War did *not* begin
with Allen Dulles' "secret 1945 negotiations with the
Nazis." Moreover, asserts Schlesinger, Soviet-American
Cold War antagonism clearly stemmed from actions
undertaken by the Stalin regime, not by the United
States.

May I submit that both historians are engaging in
futile pinpointing of the exact start of the Cold War?
That in any case Soviet-American animosity goes back
a good deal farther than April 1945?

If we must fix upon some obvious date, let me suggest that the Yalta Conference of February 1945 forms
a more convincing starting point for charting the down-
hill course in Soviet-American relations, a process which
had actually set in *during the Second World War*. As
a matter of fact, Stalin's decision to remove Browder
from the helm of the CPUSA—these still were the days
when the Kremlin could unilaterally dump foreign

Communist leaders—came just at the time of Yalta. And what happened at Yalta that demonstrates the beginning of the freeze in Soviet-American relations?

All the pent-up hostility between the United States and the USSR, shelved "for the duration," floated to the surface. The defeat of Nazi Germany loomed on the horizon, and the whole postwar settlement of Europe clearly lay before these *two* major powers in the world. This bi-polarity was thrown in relief by the weakness of both France and Britain by the end of the war. And, of course, long before Yalta, Stalin and his associates had made it abundantly clear—and not only in pontifical ideological pronunciamentos—that the Soviets considered all of Eastern Europe their exclusive bailiwick, a region to be "liberated" by the Red Army and subject to sovietization.

I recommend that both historians reread (or read carefully for the first time) Chapter XXXII of Robert E. Sherwood's *Roosevelt and Hopkins—An Intimate History*. In this chapter, entitled "Beginnings of Dissension," Sherwood, playwright and part-time historian (the best kind, evidently), details the process by which the Soviet-American "strange alliance" had deteriorated by the winter of 1944–45. Pointing to March 1945, Sherwood reports in his chapter on the Yalta Conference:

> By the middle of March 1945 a situation had developed in Rumania which indicated that the Russians were determined to set up governments in Eastern Europe in conformance with their own interpretation of the word "friendly" and without regard for the principles of the Atlantic Charter which had just been reaffirmed. . . . It was beginning to appear evident that a complete deadlock had developed among the British, Russian, and American conferees. . . . There was now a growing feeling of un-

easiness born of the unknown and the inexplicable, regarding the true relationship between the Soviet Union and the United States, Great Britain, and the other members of the United Nations. . . . It was beginning to be feared that a monstrous fraud had been perpetrated at Yalta, with Roosevelt and Churchill as the unwitting dupes.

A similar description—and dating—of the manifest worsening of Soviet-American relations may be found in George F. Kennan's *Russia and the West Under Lenin and Stalin.*

The freezing process had clearly accelerated toward the end of the European phase of World War II.

While it is clear that the Western Allies are not utterly blameless, it is even clearer that Stalin's Russia played the crucial role in initiating what came to be called the Cold War by committing or instigating political, economic, and military aggression in the 1940s and 1950s. Stalin's policy of Communist expansionism led to the formation of NATO and the Warsaw Pact Alliance—fungi thriving on the putrescence of the wartime alliance of the Soviet Union and the United States.

Albert L. Weeks

New York University

Gar Alperovitz replies:

Michael Korda is right to recall Wolff's Nazi record, above all to stress that Dulles, a high-level intelligence agent, should have been most skeptical when he was, in fact, most trusting. While Wolff dickered with him (building a "good Nazi" reputation for after the war) he simultaneously reported directly to Hitler himself.

I agree with Professor Weeks that there is little point in trying to define a precise starting date for the Cold

War. I had hoped my review suggested as much, for the Dulles episode is important not because it was a starting date but because it illustrates that we must learn to understand the Cold War as an *ongoing interaction* involving a complex series of linked actions and reactions, responses and counterresponses. "Causation" becomes a very subtle question; and the ultimate roots of all this, of course, go very deep; they can be traced at least to 1917. Nevertheless, specific events occur at specific times, and it is a fact that the first serious hostilities of what we term the Cold War occurred in March 1945. They were set off when suspicions arising from Dulles' negotiations coincided with and reinforced difficulties over the Polish issue. Interestingly, Professor Weeks pinpoints not one but two "starting dates" for the Cold War, among these March 1945.

Gar Alperovitz [Sept. 8] speaks of Allen Dulles' myopia while exhibiting a choice myopia of his own. You don't have to be Barry Goldwater to see the folly of ascribing the Cold War to our having hurt Joseph Stalin's feelings. One could come away from a reading of Professor Alperovitz's "review" believing Stalin to have been little more than a benign comrade-in-arms twitted by a United States intelligence officer's ambitions. If only we had played it square with the man, there would have been no Iron Curtain, no enslavement of Eastern Europe. He would have *trusted* us then. . . . This is the hair shirt many American liberals still like to don, but it implies a misreading of history just as simpleminded as the devil theory of Communism cherished by many American conservatives. Certainly Dulles' mission was a diplomatic boner, and certainly he should have been fired for countermanding Roosevelt's orders, but to credit him with the great tragedy of the Cold War gives him a stature, and Stalin a benevolence, that could serve only Charles de Gaulle's notions of American naïveté.

Donald Hutter

New Canaan, Connecticut

Gar Alperovitz replies to a letter from Arthur Schlesinger, Jr., and in reference to Professor Schlesinger's essay in the Autumn 1967 issue of Foreign Affairs.

Arthur Schlesinger's statement of the doctrine of historical inevitability helps set the terms of debate over the origins of the Cold War. He writes: "One thing, and one thing alone," permitted wartime Soviet-American cooperation; "nothing" could have dispelled Stalin's mistrust; "no" American policy could have won confidence; "every" American initiative was poisoned from the source. Since Stalin's "rigid theology" required him to start a battle for Europe, American activities could have played no substantial role in the beginning of the Cold War.

In my review of *The Secret Surrender* I argued neither that Allen Dulles started the Cold War nor that the United States has been responsible for everything which has gone wrong in the last twenty years. What I wrote was quite specific: "The Cold War cannot be understood *simply* as an American response to a Soviet challenge, but rather as the insidious *interaction* of mutual suspicions, blame for which must be shared by all." As an illustration I pointed out that we now have evidence that Dulles' secret 1945 negotiations with the

Nazis undermined American-Soviet relations in much the same way as did the later U-2 incident.

One approach to a discussion of differing interpretations of the Cold War is to recall the view urged by Secretary of War Henry L. Stimson in 1945. He held, contrary to Mr. Schlesinger's idea, that the United States had it in its power profoundly to influence postwar relations with the Soviet Union. This responsibility, he believed, demanded that provocative actions be avoided. Arguing against the hawks of his day—especially on European matters—Stimson urged "the greatest care and the greatest patience and the greatest thoughtfulness." By the time of his resignation, however, he had lost the debate. And on nuclear matters he was dismayed to find Secretary of State Byrnes "very much against any attempt to cooperate with Russia. . . ."

Most observers agree the major turning point of the Cold War came in 1947. What happened earlier? Stimson was aware that the tough line had won out in 1945 in the United States Government. Did this fact have consequences, or was everything inevitably fated from the start? Soviet provocations, brutality, and terror called forth American responses, but what produced Soviet policies? Why such surprising beginnings as Soviet sponsorship of the 1945 free elections in Hungary, which routed the Communists? And how account for Stalin's agreement not to aid the Greek Communists (strictly adhered to, according to Churchill)? Any study of the Cold War must go beyond current simplifications to define with precision to what extent American actions can be understood as responsive to Soviet behavior, or, on the other hand, causative of it, or both.

Serious historians of the Cold War will also have to deal with the 1945 Jacques Duclos article cited by Mr.

Schlesinger, but many will be surprised to see him offer the article as "definitive proof" of a shift in Soviet strategy toward Europe. Duclos' article did have impact in American Communist circles, precipitating both a change in party leadership and a hardening of policy. In point of fact, however, Duclos did not argue against supporting bourgeois governments, as Mr. Schlesinger has it. On the contrary, he even endorsed Communist support of Roosevelt. What he did attack was the 1944 decision of the American Communist Party to dissolve itself, and he denounced such excesses—for Marxists— as Browder's wartime embrace of "monopolistic trust" leaders like J. P. Morgan.

As for Europe, again Duclos' article had a meaning different from that ascribed to it by Mr. Schlesinger. In 1945 it was one of many confirmations that European Communists had decided to abandon violent revolutionary struggle in favor of the more modest aim of electoral success. Duclos' main point was that it would be a mistake to copy the American Communist Party's withdrawal from electoral politics. Subsequently, French and other European Communists, including Duclos, lay down the arms they had learned to use in the resistance to devote primary attention to the open political arena; and they continued to toss Marxist theology to the winds by participating in De Gaulle's and other early postwar "bourgeois" governments.

Communist policy throughout Europe was to become militant, totalitarian, and brutal, but not in response to Duclos' article, and not in 1945, but for the most part in late 1946 and during 1947. That surprising ambivalence and considerable moderation were evident in the earliest postwar years suggests a more open view of historical possibilities—and also that the Cold War may be viewed as the result of decisions made by men

in at least two nations. It may well be, as Walter Lippmann observed at the time, that "an accommodation,
a *modus vivendi*, a working arrangement, some simple
form of cooperation" was possible, but that by demanding more, United States policy got less, "making the best
the enemy of the good."

Historians are now beginning a painstaking review of
the period before Communist strategy toughened to determine precisely how American and Soviet moves in-
teracted. In this significant investigation there is need
for much research and an open and public sifting of
evidence and testing of ideas. It is disappointing and
somehow sad that an eminent member of the historical
profession should feel called upon to admonish that
"the whistle be blown" on this intellectual effort.

Diplomatic Historian

In his essay on my book, *The Atomic Bomb and the
End of World War II*, Gar Alperovitz writes that
I come "close to being our official national diplomatic
historian." I don't know how close that is supposed to
be. But I should like readers of his article to know that
this book was an entirely private and independent undertaking. No one in the government, or former member of the government, had anything to do with its in-
ception; nor did any of them pass upon the manuscript.
I was under no obligation to defer to any official or
official opinion, nor did I. No branch of the government
(not even the CIA) provided a dollar toward its production. Long before the book was begun my last connection with the government had ended.

I have the impression that Alperovitz attributes my
uncertitude about various hypothetical "options" to my

wish to spare friends or former associates. Could it be due rather to knowledge that, in decisions upon which so many considerations bore, what is known justifies only surmises, not certitudes? Sometimes decision-makers do not themselves clearly know the relative impact of the many ideas or calculations which influence them. Sometimes what may appear in the calm of the study years afterward to have been a genuine "option" at the time was not actually so in the hot flux of events.

Alperovitz also seems to impugn my judgment because of my previous personal or professional connection with some of the chief figures in the narrative. Might that rather not have caused my interpretation of complex circumstances to be closer to the whole truth than any derived from the available record, even were it impartial?

Who, if he did not know it, would gather from reading his article that a bloody and dreadful war was being fought, that each day it continued meant agony to our combatants as well as to the Japanese? Who would gather that the fanatic military leaders preferred death to acceptance of defeat?

In short, this essay illustrates how preconceptions assist hindsight; they act as a focus which selects the conclusions.

May I take this chance to state that one of my main efforts at present is to induce the American Government to make the records of the diplomacy of the recent past available to all, more quickly and fully. My latest attempt to arouse interest in the purpose is an article in the January 1967 issue of *Foreign Affairs* called "The Shackled Historian." Perhaps Alperovitz and his colleagues in the Kennedy Center will take up the cause.

Since Alperovitz, like myself, is interested in the origins of the Cold War, will he not call on the Soviet Government—which he apparently thinks was merely the hapless object of our vicious diplomacy—to do the same? Without the Soviet documents and memoirs all accounts of the Cold War must be lopsided. Were they to be published, I do not think it possible that Alperovitz could continue to write in the same vein as he does now.

Herbert Feis

York, Maine

Gar Alperovitz replies:

Herbert Feis's letter is strangely ambiguous: the trouble is that like his book it never quite faces fundamental issues squarely.

My review attempted to document three specific points about the Hiroshima decision: (1) by July 1945, before the atomic bombs were used, other courses of action seemed likely to end the war well in advance of the planned November landing; (2) this is true not merely in retrospect: we now know that a variety of other courses was offered directly to the President by his highest official advisers before Hiroshima—at a time when he was also shown intercepted cables revealing Japan's willingness to end the war on acceptable terms; (3) the main reason other possibilities were passed up appears to be that implicitly or explicitly a demonstration of America's new power was judged necessary to strengthen the United States hand against Russia. The bomb was a "master card" of diplomacy, in the words of Secretary Stimson: it would make Russia more "manageable," according to Secretary Byrnes.

Characteristically, Mr. Feis does not directly dispute

135

any of the documents, facts, or arguments offered in support of this view.

Neither do his comments about Soviet documents relate to the main point at issue (although, of course, as a historian I welcome his efforts to obtain further historical materials).

When Mr. Feis does touch on a point of substance he does so in a curiously defensive way. I mentioned his official connections and privileged access to inside information not to impugn his motives. Rather I wished mainly to stress that an established historian—not an ill-informed layman, not an inflammatory publicist—has reached important new conclusions about Hiroshima: it is significant that an expert of Mr. Feis's stature—who has private information not available to other scholars —has come to understand there were other ways to end the war. And he has written that President Truman "probably," and Secretaries Stimson and Byrnes "certainly," viewed the bomb as a way to bolster the United States diplomatic position against Russia.

In sum, Feis's book marks a major shift in the accepted view of America's use of the first atomic bomb (although the shift is unfortunately shrouded in rather vague phrases). My review attempted to cut through to underlying evidence to show that considerations related to Russia were absolutely central to the Hiroshima decision. His response, I had hoped, might contain documented, expert objections. Regrettably, however, his general remarks about preconceptions and hindsight once again define a position of ambiguity. We are left to puzzle whether Mr. Feis is withholding such objections as he has or whether, in fact, he holds no substantive objections at all.

VIII. BIBLIOGRAPHIC NOTE

For those who wish to read further into the revisionist approach to American history, the following is a very brief list of major books.

ALPEROVITZ, GAR. *Atomic Diplomacy: Hiroshima and Potsdam* (New York: Vintage, 1965).

BARNET, RICHARD. *Intervention and Revolution: America's Confrontation with Insurgent Movements Around the World* (New York: New American Library, 1968).

BARNET, RICHARD and RASKIN, MARCUS. *After 20 Years* (New York: Random House, 1965).

DONNELLY, DESMOND. *Struggle for the World. The Cold War: 1917–1965* (New York: St. Martins, 1965).

FLEMING, D. F. *The Cold War and Its Origins, 1917–60* (New York: Doubleday, 1961).

———. *The Origins and Legacy of World War I* (New York: Doubleday, 1968).

HALLE, LOUIS J. *The Cold War as History* (New York: Harper & Row, 1967).

HEILBRONER, ROBERT. *New Empire: An Interpretation of American Expansion, 1860–1898* (Ithaca: Cornell University Press, 1967).

HOROWITZ, DAVID, ed. *Containment and Revolution* (Boston: Beacon Press, 1967).

KOLKO, GABRIEL. *The Politics of War: The World and United States Foreign Policy, 1943–1945* (New York: Random House, 1969).

——. *Triumph of Conservatism* (Chicago: Quadrangle, 1967).

——. *The Roots of American Foreign Policy* (Boston: Beacon Press, 1969).

LAFEBER, WALTER. *America, Russia, and the Cold War, 1945–66* (New York: John Wiley & Sons, 1967).

MAYER, ARNO J. *Political Origins of the New Diplomacy, 1917–18* (New York: Fertig, 1959).

——. *Politics and Diplomacy of Peacemaking: Containment and Counter-Revolution at Versailles, 1918–1919* (New York: Knopf, 1968).

——. *Wilson vs. Lenin: Political Origins of the New Diplomacy, 1917–18* (New York: Meridian, World Publishing, 1967).

OGLESBY, CARL, and SHAULL, RICHARD. *Containment and Change: Two Dissenting Views of American Society and Foreign Policy in the New Revolutionary Age* (New York: Macmillan, 1968).

WILLIAMS, WILLIAM APPLEMAN. *Contours of American History* (Chicago: Quadrangle, 1966).

——. *Great Evasion* (Chicago: Quadrangle, 1968).

——. *Shaping of American Diplomacy* (Chicago: Rand McNally, 1956).

——. *The Tragedy of American Diplomacy* (New York: Dell, 1968).

——. *The Roots of the American Empire* (New York: Random House, 1969).

INDEX

Acheson, Dean, 11–12, 23
Aid. *See* Economic aid
Airey, Gen. Terence, 30
Alanbrooke, Lord, 69
Alexander, Field Marshal
    Harold, 30
Algeria, 106
Alliance for Progress, 79
Antirevolutionary policies.
    See Diplomacy
Armistice agreements
    (1944), 39–40
Arnold, Gen. Henry H., 62
Atomic bombs
    Russians explode (1949),
      8
    U.S. explodes (1945), 68
    See also Nuclear power
Atomic Energy Commission,
    $60n$, 66
Austria, 45, 81

Bailey, Thomas A., 83
Bard, Ralph, 61
Barnes, Harry, 104
Barnes, Maynard, 97
Barnet, Richard, 81, $92n$
Baruch, Bernard, 8
Batista, Fulgencio, 83, 103
Bay of Pigs invasion (1961),
    25, 33
Beard, Charles, 104
Berlin blockade (1948), 8
Bernadotte, Count, 26
"Berne Incident," 14, 25–33
Bernstein, Barton J., $84n$
Blackett, P. M. S., 66
Blockade
    Berlin (1948), 8
    of Japan, 52–53
Bohr, Niels, $67n$
Boxer Rebellion (1900), 80
Bradley, Gen. Omar, 116

15 L

Kolko, Gabriel, 18, 100–1, 121*n*
Konoye, Prince, 54–55
Korea, 78
Korean war, 115–16
Kyushu (Japan), 53, 54, 60

Lafeber, Walter, 92*n*
Lane, Arthur Bliss, 98
Laos, 78
Lasch, Christopher, 7–23
Leahy, Adm. William, 63, 111
Lebanon, 78
Left, U.S. and, 76
LeMay, Gen. Curtis, 62–63
Lemnitzer, Gen. Lyman L., 30
Lend-Lease (1945), 98
Lippmann, Walter, 36–37, 103

MacArthur, Gen. Douglas, 64, 116
McCarthy, Eugene, 117
McCarthy, Joseph, 8
McCloy, John, 60
McNeill, William, 9
Manhattan Project, 60*n*
Marshall, Gen. George C., 58, 64
Marshall Plan, 10
Marx, Karl, 49
Marxism, 85
Marzani, Carl, 10
Masaryk, Jan, 99
Mayer, Arno, 81
Metaxas, John, 103
Mexican Revolution, 81, 82

Mexico, 81, 82, 83
Michael (King of Rumania), 96
Mikolajczyk, Stanislaw, 98
Military bureaucracy
counterrevolution and, 75–76
use of atomic bomb and, 62–63
Military intervention, 80–84
Molotov, V., 29, 73*n*
Dulles' negotiations and, 27–28
meets Truman, 67–68
Munich agreement (1938), 84

Nagasaki (Japan), 63, 67, 73
New Left, 85, 90
Nicaragua, 80, 82, 83
Nixon, Richard M., 91, 118
Nkrumah, Kwame, 79
NATO (North Atlantic Treaty Organization), 8
Nuclear power
Churchill and. *See* Churchill, Winston
political use of, 13, 14, 43, 51–73, 110–12
advocated, 64–65
opposition to using bomb, 14, 62–64, 66, 68–73
political motives, 65–73
reasons for using bomb, 58–61
"shock options" and, 59, 61–62